# THE HISTORY OF WALES

## J. GRAHAM JONES

CARDIFF
UNIVERSITY OF WALES PRESS
2014

First published in 1990
Reprinted in 1991, 1992, 1993, 1995, 1997

Second edition published in 1998
Reprinted in 2000, 2005

Third edition published in 2014

*www.uwp.co.uk*

*British Library Cataloguing-in-Publication Data*
A catalogue record for this book is available from the British Library.

ISBN   978-1-78316-168-3
eISBN   978-1-78316-169-0

Printed by CPI Antony Rowe, Chippenham, Wiltshire

# Contents

# Acknowledgements

The author and publishers wish to thank the copyright holders who have kindly permitted the reproduction of photographs as follows:—

Pentre Ifan (p. 2), Caernarfon Castle (p. 43), The Parliament House, Machynlleth (p. 52), Gwydir (p. 75), Capel Soar-y-Mynydd (p. 94), University College of Wales, Aberystwyth (p. 137), Senedd Debating Chamber (p. 188) and Millennium Stadium (p. 200) by permission of the Photolibrary Wales. Glamorgan Colliery (p. 117) and Ceremony of the Gorsedd of Bards (p. 142) by permission of Alamy. Map of Wales in 1267 (p. 31), Wales in 1284 (p. 38) and the Shires of Wales after the Acts of Union (p. 57), from T. Herbert and G. E. Jones (eds), *Edward I and Tudor Wales*, by permission of the Open University in Wales. The title-page of the 1588 Bible (p. 67) by permission of Llyfrgell Genedlaethol Cymru/The National Library of Wales. Map of the counties and districts of Wales in 1974 (p. 171), drawn by Welsh Office Cartographic Services, based on an Ordnance Survey map, by kind permission of Ordnance Survey © Crown Copyright. NC/04/37793.

# Preface to the First Edition

This little book is simply an attempt to outline some of the main themes in the history of Wales. The attempt has not been made, as far as I am aware, since Sir John Edward Lloyd, doyen of Welsh historians, published his *A History of Wales* in the Benn's Sixpenny Library Series in 1930. Since then, and especially during the last twenty-five years, the study of Welsh history has enjoyed a quite remarkable renaissance, the fruits of which are at once apparent in the magisterial volumes of the Oxford History of Wales.

Within the constraints of space upon me, I have been unable to discuss many aspects of our rich and colourful past and have dealt only briefly with others to which I would gladly have devoted more attention. In particular, I am painfully aware that the few references to Welsh literature which the volume contains are woefully sketchy and inadequate.

In this book the county names in use between 1974 and 1996 have been used wherever more appropriate (see map on p. 171) but for the period 1536–1974 references are to the historical county names (see map on p. 57).

A number of my colleagues in the Department of Manuscripts and Records of the National Library of Wales have generously assisted me in various ways in the preparation of the book, and I should like to mention in particular Mrs Eirionedd Baskerville, Mr Daniel Huws and Mr Graham Thomas. My friend Dr Prys T. J. Morgan, Reader in History at the University College of Swansea, at a particularly busy time read through the whole of my typescript with characteristic speed and penetration and did much to eliminate factual errors and to improve my cumbersome prose. The errors of fact and interpretation which remain are, of course, my own responsibility.

Finally my thanks are due to the staff of the University of Wales Press, especially Mr John Rhys and Mrs Ceinwen Jones, for every assistance and co-operation.

J. GRAHAM JONES
September 1989
Department of Manuscripts and Records
National Library of Wales
Aberystwyth

# Preface to the Second Edition

*A Pocket Guide: The History of Wales* was first published in 1990. It has been reprinted five times, and so I have already corrected minor errors and inaccuracies; I am most grateful to friends and reviewers, most notably Emeritus Professor Sir Glanmor Williams, for noting some of them. In this new edition I have also updated the final chapter by outlining briefly events in the 1990s and have revised the guide to further reading and the list of important dates. Generally, I did not feel it necessary to modify the main text as originally written in 1988–9, and I am much gratified by the reception accorded to the first edition and its successive reprints.

As always, it is a pleasure to record my gratitude to the University of Wales Press, especially Susan Jenkins, for unfailing ready support and ever tolerant forbearance.

J. Graham Jones
May 1998
Department of Manuscripts and Records
National Library of Wales
Aberystwyth

# Preface to the Third Edition

Sixteen long and eventful years have passed by since the revision and publication of the second edition of this little book which has, unfortunately, been unavailable in print for several years. I have, therefore, decided to add an additional chapter briefly outlining the events and trends of this crowded, exciting period in our recent history. I have also updated the table of important dates and the guide to further reading. I very much hope that these will prove helpful and stimulating to a new generation of readers and students of Welsh history.

As always, I am most indebted to the staff of the University of Wales Press, especially Dr Llion Wigley, for so readily agreeing to re-publish the book in this new attractive format, and for unfailing editorial assistance and ready support.

J. Graham Jones
Aberystwyth
May 2014

# 1

# Pre-Norman Wales

## *The earliest inhabitants*

There is some evidence of human habitation in Wales as long ago as 250,000 BC. But positive remains date only from late Palaeolithic times (*c.*50,000–8,000 BC) and show that the people were cave-dwellers. The rock-shelters and small caves in which these primitive hunters lived include the Cae-gwyn cave near St Asaph, Paviland in Gower, Coygan in southern Dyfed and the Cat's Hole in west Dyfed. They existed in abysmally cold conditions and hunted oxen, reindeer and other wild animals with primitive stone weapons. Certainly, the Palaeolithic population was thinly spread and culturally impoverished; none of the high-quality cave art which flourished in France and Spain was to be found in Wales, which remained on the very fringe of civilization.

### Stone-Age caves

The caves which show evidence of occupation in late Palaeolithic or Neolithic times are the oldest human dwelling places and tombs in Wales which we can now identify. Some are now protected as monuments of the earliest human inhabitants of Wales. The most famous is the 'Goat's Hole', Paviland (Gower), in which were found a large number of stone tools and a headless skeleton of a youth ritually buried about 18,000 years ago. The skeleton had been stained with red ochre and became popularly and inaccurately known as the 'Red Lady'.

## *Mesolithic man*

About 6,000 BC the British Isles separated from the mainland of Europe. By this time new immigrants had arrived – called Mesolithic or Middle Stone Age folk – but in Wales their civilization remained primitive. Their weapons were simple, and they fished on the shores and hunted on the fringes of the great forests which had sprung up in the warmer and wetter climate. They were able to make tools from stone, bone and particularly flint. It has been estimated that the number of these people in Wales was very small, perhaps no more than about 300.

## *Neolithic man*

Technology improved as fresh waves of settlers arrived. More advanced cultivation and domesticated farm animals evolved in the Middle East around 9,000 BC. These techniques spread

*Pentre Ifan burial chamber, near Nevern, Dyfed, a stone-built Neolithic tomb.*

westwards in a number of ways – of greatest significance to Wales were the routes which passed through the Mediterranean basin, along the coasts of Atlantic Europe and via the western seas – and may not have reached Wales until about 3,000 BC, when there is evidence of the use of improved stone axes, the construction of massive stone-built tombs, and the adoption of the practice of herding animals. At around this time cultivation of the land first took place in Wales.

## Neolithic remains

Some Neolithic communities in Britain built oblong houses, with ridge roofs carried on rows of posts. Examples have been found at Newton Nottage near Porthcawl and Clegyr Boia near St David's. The burial chamber at Tinkinswood in South Glamorgan is a large trapezoid at the north-eastern end of a cairn 130 feet long and 60 feet wide. It was excavated and partially restored in 1914. The chamber is enclosed on three sides by upright slabs, while a single great capstone weighing about 40 tons forms the roof. It contained the bones of about fifty individuals and pottery resembling that made in southern England. There are similar chambers at St Lythans near Tinkinswood, now completely exposed, at Parc le Breos, Gower, and at Capel Garmon, Clwyd, overlooking the upper Conwy valley. The round cairns of the type found in northern Ireland and south-west Scotland have been found in north-west and west Wales. The best preserved is at Trefnigath, Holyhead, originally 45 feet long and comprising four chambers. The Pentre Ifan 'Cromlech', near Nevern in south Dyfed (the best-known of all Welsh megalithic monuments) has attracted attention by the height of its great capstone under which it was possible for a man to ride on horseback. There remains today the skeleton of a single oblong chamber with a capstone 16 feet long.

Many Neolithic men lived in caves; others existed in open settlements on spurs of land near the coast. Their dwellings were made of wood and have not survived. The use of metal had not yet penetrated to north-west Europe, but implements have been found dating from this period which were ground and polished, made from the abundant supply of the tough and durable igneous rock in Wales. June 1919 saw the discovery at Penmaen-mawr in north Gwynedd of the remains of a 'great axe factory' of Neolithic times. Axes made at Penmaen-mawr have been found as far afield as Wiltshire, south Scotland and northern Ireland. Such discoveries bear witness to a marked freedom of movement and trade.

The great stones of the burial chambers of Neolithic man still stand, towering and majestic, after 4,000 years. Some are round and others long in plan. A fine example of one of the long cairns survives at Tinkinswood, St Nicholas, on the coastal plain of Glamorgan. Large numbers of round cairns are to be found in Anglesey. It is evident from these tombs and from the production of tools that Neolithic man lived in substantial communities, believed in a god and possessed a rudimentary knowledge of engineering.

## The Bronze Age

The Beaker folk, who originated in Spain, first sailed into Britain about 2,000 BC. They buried their dead in single graves adorned by a distinctive 'waisted' earthenware pot or beaker. No more than thirty of these have been discovered in Wales, scattered along the coastal plains of the north and south or in the Severn, Wye and Usk valleys – all easily invaded from the east or the sea. They largely failed to penetrate into the western highlands which remained the preserve of the Neolithic people. It was the Beaker folk who introduced metal-working into Britain, as is evidenced by the gold, copper and bronze objects found in their graves. But stone generally remained in use for rough tools, now more imaginatively adapted to the flint dagger, the axe-hammer and the arrow head. The Presely hills in Dyfed provided much of the stone for the great circle of Stonehenge in Wiltshire, and a dozen smaller circles built during this period have been discovered within Wales, all of them on the uplands. Numbers of food vessels have also survived, mostly found on the coastal plains.

A sudden development in the use of bronze occurred after about 1,000 BC, when the first Celts reached the south coasts of Britain.

The number and variety of metal tools increased dramatically. Many distribution points for bronze tools have been identified in Wales. People began to clear areas of forest for farming and a substantial increase in the population of Wales took place. People lived further inland, surviving by keeping herds of sheep, pigs and oxen. Crops were raised on the rich soil of the plains.

## The Iron Age

The Celts had mastered improved techniques of iron-working and more advanced farming skills such as a two-oxen plough and iron ploughshare. It is during Iron Age B, c. 300–100 BC, that the roots of a distinctive Welsh life and culture can be detected. Low-land agricultural villages were built up, and large numbers of hill-forts were built, especially along the south-west and west coasts and in the border area. A more pastoral economy developed in Wales; wheat, barley and flax were grown in small enclosures, and a number of domestic animals kept. Perhaps the hill-forts were used only for protection during the frequent bouts of strife rather than as permanent homes. Sophisticated iron and bronze implements were widespread and decorated ornaments, weapons and pottery provide evidence of high artistic quality. Yet these people lived crudely, indeed savagely. The squalor of the hill-forts contrasts strikingly with the examples of their highly developed artistic skill.

### Iron-Age forts

Most of the prehistoric fortifications in Wales belong to the early Iron Age, to the last five or six centuries before the Roman conquest. By this time there had developed an elaborate tradition of dry-stone rampart building, with timber-framing used on a large scale. These forts were usually sited on isolated hills, the defences following the contours all around. Elaborate systems of defence at entrances developed. Caer y Twr, near Holyhead on Anglesey, covers an area of some seventeen acres on the highest part of Holyhead Mountain, and consists of a simple dry-stone rampart. On the north side it is

13 feet thick and up to 10 feet high. Two hill-forts in Gwent – Llanmelin and the Bulwarks, Chepstow – have closely sited, multiple ramparts. The former was laid out as a contour fort with a mesh of ramparts and ditches continuing all around it without interruption. It may have been the tribal capital of the Silures before the Roman conquest. The Bulwarks Camp, Chepstow, is a small promontory hill-fort, originally defended by a double bank and ditch. It enclosed no more than 1.5 acres and was regarded as a strongly defended homestead. The sloping-fronted multiple ramparts again suggest construction in the immediate pre-Roman period.

## The Welsh language

In their homeland the Celts employed a tongue spoken over a wide area, now termed Common Celtic, a language which divided into two main groups: Goidelic and Brittonic. The Welsh language was eventually to descend from the Brittonic group. Certainly, the Iron-Age people spoke Celtic languages when they reached the British Isles. Goidelic-speakers occupied the north of Scotland, the Isle of Man and Ireland, while Brittonic took root in Wales, England and the south of Scotland. Considerable intermixture inevitably followed, and Goidelic was probably spoken in some parts of Wales, particularly in the north-west and the south-west. It was to be greatly strengthened by extensive Irish settlement in the immediate post-Roman period.

## Roman Wales

The Emperor Claudius invaded Britain in AD 43 in an urgent attempt to secure the north-west frontier of the Roman Empire. Most of the south of England was subdued by the Roman legions within five years. Shortly after AD 70 the Romans began to build the fortresses which were to serve as permanent bases for their legions and to facilitate the control of the military zones in Wales, Scotland and the north of England. Deva (Chester) and Isca Silurum (Caerleon) were begun in AD 74 and served as the major garrison towns of Wales. Each held some 6,000 legionaries – heavily armed and well-paid foot-soldiers. Some twenty-four small forts were constructed and linked by hundreds of miles of specially built roads. Some of these fort sites in Wales carry the element *caer* (castle or fort) in their place-names today, among them Caerhun, Caersŵs, and Pen-y-gaer. The Roman conquest of Wales, though fraught with difficulties, was speedily accomplished by AD 78. But it did not in any way transform the lives of the Celtic peoples. While some tribes, such as the Silures in south-east Wales, were moved into recently constructed Roman towns, many smaller groups pursued their traditional way of life undisturbed. Roman Wales always remained a frontier zone. Anglesey was to prove a particular source of resistance; here was the headquarters of the Druids, a cult hated by the Romans.

Three centuries of Roman occupation certainly bequeathed a legacy to Wales. A new element was added to the population of the country; improved agrarian practices were introduced, especially in the Vale of Glamorgan where numbers of large villas were established; more sophisticated mining technology was practised in the search for minerals: gold, iron, copper and lead. Large numbers of Latin words entered everyday speech. Roman pottery and trinkets passed from the hands of the Roman soldiers to those of the natives. Although, when the last Eagle Standard of the Roman legions left Wales permanently in AD 383, the life of the Celtic peoples continued much as before, there was a permanent legacy to the people and landscape of Wales. The roads, forts, dykes and watermills stood as models of engineering, often serving right through to the nineteenth century.

## Roman forts

The Roman army, ever methodical, laid out the sites of its forts by means of a cross-staff set up in the middle of the cleared area. The stone fort at Gelligaer shows that a standard measuring-staff of 10 Roman feet was employed in setting out the buildings. They were designed for a professional army, neatly planned and oblong in shape, the size closely related to the numbers in the garrison envisaged. Caerleon covers about fifty acres, designed for a legion 5,300 strong. Roman forts have the same basic layout: the area was divided laterally into three by streets. The central part contained the headquarters, usually flanked by the commandant's house, construction shop and a pair of granaries holding a two-year supply. The front and rear divisions, bisected by streets leading to gates, were largely given up to barracks and stabling. The forts had ramparts of earth strengthened with timber or stone and fronted by ditches on the outer side. Much of this arrangement survives at Segontium on the outskirts of Caernarfon, begun about AD 78 and rebuilt in stone twenty years later. It was excavated by Sir Mortimer Wheeler in the 1920s, and many of the relics he excavated are to be found in a small museum. At Castell Collen built by the Romans on the road leading from their fort at Brecon the banks, ditches and some stonework can still be traced. The remains of gateways can still be seen at Segontium, Brecon Gaer and Neath, while Caerleon Amphitheatre, dating from about AD 80, has been fully excavated. Many of the finds from the numerous excavations at Caerleon are housed in the Legionary Museum near the church.

## Cunedda Wledig

Soon after the withdrawal of the Romans, advancing barbarian peoples entered Britain. From the fifth century they pushed to the north and to the west and thus isolated the Celts of Wales from the other Celtic peoples. It was at this time that Wales became a tangible territorial unit. The Welsh were confined, restricted and under attack, particularly by the Irish on the west and the Picts on the north. The Welsh folk-tales in *The Mabinogion* often refer to the constant coming and going between Wales and Ireland. Colonies of Irish folk had long since settled in Dyfed and in Llŷn, but the invaders who followed the collapse of Rome were fierce pirates rather than peaceful settlers.

Tradition records that, at the beginning of the fifth century, Cunedda Wledig and his sons left Manaw Gododdin (a settlement in the country of the Otadini, along the banks of the Firth of Forth, near North Berwick and Edinburgh, and one of the Brythonic kingdoms of north Britain) for Gwynedd (north-west Wales), where they expelled the Irish settlers and founded their own dynasty, their descendants ruling as the royal house of Gwynedd. This tradition, recorded in the *Historia Brittonum* of Nennius (a compilation of historical and geographical lore dating from about AD 800), is at least partly confirmed by the evidence of Goidelic features in north-west Wales. Einion Yrth, Cunedda's eldest son, is credited with the defeat of the Irish and the consolidation of Welsh influence in the north-west. Cunedda, we are told, was accompanied by eight sons, who gave their names to many of the regions of north and west Wales, among them Ceredig-ion, Rhufon-iog and Edeirn-ion, while the name of his grandson took root in Meirion-nydd.

## The other Welsh kingdoms

Cunedda was not the father of all the Welsh kingdoms. Irish influences were even more marked in south-west Wales than in the north-west. This may be attributed to the migration of Goidelic people from the land of the Deisi in southern Ireland in the fourth and fifth centuries. The royal dynasty which emerged in Pembroke or Dyfed in the extreme south-west was clearly of Irish origins. Yet an inscribed stone commemorating a sixth-century ruler styled 'Voteporix the Protector' suggests the presence, too, of Romano-British characteristics. The small inland kingdom of Brycheiniog (or Brecon) nurtured a dynasty which claimed descent from a native princess and an Irish prince from Pembroke or even from Ireland itself. Perhaps this explains why Brycheiniog, together with southern Dyfed, has more inscriptions in the Irish alphabet called Ogam – seven in all – than any other part of Wales.

In the south-east of Wales, where the urban communities of the Romans were most firmly established, stable kingdoms emerged somewhat later. Here Glywysing and Gwent came together in the seventh century to form Morgannwg. Finally, a large area in north-central Wales formed the kingdom of Powys, which may have enjoyed an unbroken development from Roman times. Its name derived from the *paganses*, the country people, of the state of the Cornavii upon the Welsh borderland. Centred at Pengwern upon the River Severn, the geographical location of this kingdom of Powys ensured that it was to bear the brunt of the Anglo-Saxon penetration of Wales.

The migration of Cunedda inevitably exercised a linguistic influence, eventually consolidating the hold of the Brittonic language on Wales by pushing out the Goidelic speakers. Anglo-Saxon pressure westwards in the sixth and seventh centuries meant that Celtic-speakers in Wales were isolated from their fellows in Cornwall, the north of England and Scotland. Some crossed the channel to north-west Gaul and formed the nucleus of the Breton nation. The emergence of two families of distinct and separate Celtic languages began at about this time.

## *Early Christianity*

In Wales Christianity had certainly taken root long before missions from Rome converted the pagan Anglo-Saxons in the seventh and eighth centuries. An episcopal tradition deriving from the heyday of imperial Rome survived in the non-pagan lands not conquered by the Anglo-Saxons. Moreover, ideas from the Middle East stressing the eremitical tradition – withdrawing from the world and living the life of a recluse – had been absorbed by the Church of Gaul and conveyed to Wales by Gaulish aristocratic refugees fleeing along the western sea routes in the face of the barbarian invasions. Finally, the conversion of Ireland by St Patrick and others created a vigorous source of religious energy which came to Wales, as is reflected in the Ogam inscriptions found along the western seaboard and especially in the south-east. These influences came together in the evangelical wandering missionaries called the Celtic saints, who travelled extensively through Wales preaching and converting. In areas of success they founded churches which they surrounded by earthen embankments, which defined a religious enclosure or *llan*, a word later used for the church building. The dedications of the churches reveal the spheres of influence or cult-areas of the individual saints. Many churches attracted settlements and provided Wales with its most common place-name type – *Llan* followed by the name of a saint as in Llanddewi, Llanbadarn and Llanilltud, of each of which there are numerous examples. Welsh saints were frequently associated with holy wells, many of them natural springs, sometimes with medicinal properties. The surviving remains from this early period are few, but the use of Ffynnon Gybi at Llangybi, Gwynedd, St Winifred's Chapel, Holywell, Clwyd, and the chapel of St Non, south of St David's, may reach back to the sixth or seventh centuries.

### Dewi Sant (St David)

Very little is known for certain about the patron saint of Wales, who lived in the sixth century. He may have died in 589. Most of what is believed about him is derived from the *Life* written by Rhigyfarch in Latin towards the end of the eleventh century, where it is stated that he was the son of Non and Sant. Dewi was educated at Hen Fynyw, near Aberaeron, and at Llanddeusant, and went on a pilgrimage through much of south Wales and the west of England, eventually settling at Glyn Rhosyn or St David's where he established a community leading a strict ascetic life. He went on a pilgrimage to Jerusalem where he was consecrated 'Archbishop'. A large number of feats and miracles were attributed to him. This fame spread rapidly to Ireland and to Brittany from the twelfth century, when St David's Cathedral became a popular place of pilgrimage. St David's Day, 1 March, became a Welsh national festival during the eighteenth century.

### Sculptured crosses

Stone crosses are the only monuments which have survived from the 'clasau' or monasteries of the age of conversion. Many are memorials placed over graves in the cemeteries often attached to the greater monasteries. Burial in the cemeteries was a privilege much sought after by prominent laymen. At Llantwit Major a number of these crosses are preserved, including one set up by King Hywel of Morgannwg (who ruled at the end of the ninth century) for his father Rhys. The Margam Stones Museum has a number of similar crosses. They were used in Wales down to the twelfth century. Those set up outside the south transept of Strata Florida church to commemorate Welsh princes and others date from after 1164 when the abbey was founded. Crosses erected within the 'clas' to serve as the focus of devotion or to record events in the history of the community were common in early Wales. The cross of Cynfelyn at Margam is datable by its ornament to about 900. There are fairly complete crosses in many Welsh churches, including Penally, Penmon, Diserth and Llanrhaeadr-ym-Mochnant. Some were erected to mark church property and paths. One at Carew stands over 13 feet high and bears the name of Maredudd ap Edwin, King of Deheubarth, 1033–5. The Pillar of Eliseg, which gives its name to the valley in Iâl in Clwyd, has a ninth-century origin and records the pedigree of Cyngen, the last king of Powys of the old line, who died in Rome in 854.

## Wales and the Anglo-Saxons

The Wales of the Dark Ages was a miniature chess-board of small, independent kingdoms, each ruled by its own dynasty which passed on kingship from father to son. Many of these kingdoms survived intact for a number of centuries, their ruling families enjoying a stable life of more than five hundred years. Yet Wales never succeeded in becoming a single political unit at this time and the story of the evolution of individual kingdoms is complex and difficult. Two facts are striking: there were a few continuously prominent kingdoms – the Llŷn peninsula and Anglesey in the north-west, the St David's peninsula in the south-west, the rich lands of Gwent and the Vale of Glamorgan, and the low-lands of the north-east and middle borderland. Secondly, the kingdom of Gwynedd in the north-west enjoyed a prominence which surpassed the others; it was considered the centre of resistance to the English and became the heartland of Welsh political identity.

### The legend of Arthur

Arthur was a British chieftain or military leader of the late fifth and early sixth centuries who, by the Middle Ages, had become the focus of a large corpus of tales and romances. There is but little historical evidence for his existence. He may have been the victorious commander at the Battle of Badonic Hill in c. 519 when the Britons gained a great victory over the Saxons. Geoffrey of Monmouth's *Historia* of c. 1136 gives a prominent place to Arthur's 'history', depicting Arthur as a medieval feudal emperor who had conquered the Roman armies and held court at Caerleon on the River Usk. This highly heroic portrayal of Arthur became widely known in Wales in the Middle Ages. He became the subject of a new romantic interest in the eighteenth and nineteenth centuries.

The increasing pressure exerted to the west by the Anglo-Saxon rulers who reigned in England fostered a heightened sense of Welsh national identity. When the Saxons were victorious at Dyrham in Gloucestershire in 577, the Welsh were cut off from their fellow Celts or Britons in Cornwall and the south-west, and similarly from the 'Celts' of Cumbria in 616 after the defeat of the Welsh at the Battle of Chester. In the mid-eighth century King Offa the Great of Mercia built his great dyke, thus establishing a compromise frontier with the 'Celts' of Wales and providing the Welsh with a firm eastern boundary line which stretched 149 miles from sea to sea for the first time in their history. Offa's Dyke was perhaps the most striking man-made boundary in the whole of western Europe.

### Offa's Dyke

Relations between England and Wales in the Dark Ages are represented on the ground by a number of linear earthworks – banks and ditches designed to protect the settlements of the English farmers of the kingdom of Mercia. Wat's Dyke was built in the time of King Ethelbald (716–57) and included land in dispute. Offa's Dyke, constructed about fifty years later, represented the final effort to define the whole western frontier of Mercia. It is 149 miles long from Prestatyn in Clwyd to Sedbury on the Severn Estuary, just east of the

Wye. It consists of a bank of earth, ditched generally on the west side, with an average height of some six feet and an average overall width of some sixty feet across bank and ditch. Although the design and construction were purely English, Offa's Dyke represented an agreed frontier with the Welsh. Today, after more than 1,000 years, much of it remains the boundary line between Wales and England.

Traditionally, emphasis has been placed on the enmity and almost continuous warfare among the kingdoms of Wales. In reality, however, they reveal a history of peaceful development, of gradual unification by policy and by a series of royal marriages. At the end of the eighth century fierce Norsemen or Vikings terrorized the seas and launched savage attacks upon Britain and Ireland. Wales by nature was particularly open to their attacks. The terror they aroused led to greater readiness in England and Wales to unite under strong leaders. This process of 'unification' began in ninth-century Wales under Merfyn Frych, King of Gwynedd, and his son Rhodri Mawr.

### Rhodri Mawr

Rhodri's achievements were impressive – he united much of Wales under his rule and he kept the Norsemen at bay. He succeeded to the kingdom of Powys in 855 on the death of his uncle, and a diplomatic marriage added a wide area of west Wales to his lands. This consolidation was an outstanding achievement, secured in the face of the growing power of the Saxons in the east and the new menace of the Vikings in the west. In 856, off Anglesey, Rhodri killed Gorm, the leader of the Viking fleet, a victory which brought applause from the Frankish king Charles the Bald. Rhodri was himself killed in battle against the English in 878.

The chronology of his achievements is significant. He had provided much of Wales with a brief period of unity the like of which was previously unknown. Shortly after Rhodri's death, a fundamental change occurred in the political composition of

England, a change which was to have a profound effect upon Wales. During the reigns of Alfred the Great (d. 899), Edward the Elder (d. 924) and Athelstan (d. 939), England developed from being, like Wales, a land of many kingdoms, into a single kingdom. A single monarchy was established and a centralized political structure forged. The potential for unification within Wales may have surpassed that within England, but the Welsh achievement was short-lived.

Rhodri left six sons among whom his territories were divided. It is evident that all six were regarded as a threat by the lesser kings of the south – the rulers of Dyfed, Brycheiniog, Glywysing and Gwent, who faced pressure both from Rhodri's sons and from Mercia. By a formal commendation, therefore, these rulers voluntarily entered into allegiance, individually and directly, to the English monarchy, an allegiance which was ultimately expressed in terms of homage and fealty. Rhodri's sons subsequently submitted to Alfred and in so doing completed the theoretical subjection of the Welsh kingdoms to the English monarchy.

## Hywel Dda

Rhodri's grandson, Hywel ap Cadell (Hywel Dda, 'the Good') began with a patrimony in Seisyllwg, then secured Dyfed by marriage, thus creating the kingdom of Deheubarth. Eventually he also ruled Gwynedd and Powys, thus repeating the feat of his grandfather. But he too accepted the position of a *sub-regulus*, or under-king, from Athelstan, King of Wessex, and it seems that he attempted to copy the advanced institutions of the West Saxon kingdom. Indeed, Hywel's appeasement of Athelstan provoked a reaction manifested in the poem *Armes Prydein* which dates from about 930 and which depicts the formation of an alliance of Celtic peoples to oppose the Anglo-Saxon *mechdeyrn* or over-lord, a foretaste of a theme prominent in the history of Wales throughout the medieval period. It is of significance that on contemporary English charters Hywel's signature always took precedence over those of the other Welsh kings. Hywel's name is closely linked with the codification of Welsh medieval law. It is known that he visited Rome in 928 while in the prime of life. The earliest coin struck by a Welsh king bears the legend *Hywel Rex*. Hywel's achievements were very real; during much of his long reign Wales enjoyed unity within, friendship with England and peace from the Norsemen.

## Maredudd ab Owain

The period between the death of Hywel in 950 and the accession of Gruffydd ap Llywelyn in 1039 is one of confusion. After Hywel's death Wales once again became a nation of warring kingdoms facing threats from both the English and the Norsemen. Much of the war and faction was the result of attempts by individual kings to re-establish the supremacy which Rhodri and Hywel had enjoyed. Hywel's grandson Maredudd ab Owain was the most successful. Between 986 and 999 he ruled Deheubarth, Gwynedd and Powys, although throughout his reign facing the relentless enmity of his dispossessed kinsmen in Gwynedd. Yet Maredudd's death on the eve of the millennium heralded once again a further period of anarchy. In such an age new men, not of the established dynasties, saw opportunities for advancement. These included Rhydderch ap Iestyn, who ruled Deheubarth from 1023 to 1033, Aeddan ap Blegywryd, who reigned in Gwynedd for some years until he was killed in 1018 by Llywelyn ap Seisyll, who was himself killed five years later. The prolonged internal turmoil of this period was complicated and intensified by Anglo-Saxon and Norse intervention.

### Cyfraith Hywel Dda

This is the traditional name for the native laws of Wales which are preserved in some eighty Welsh and Latin manuscripts dating from between the twelfth and eighteenth centuries. The Law Books themselves refer to a convention held at Tŷ Gwyn (at Hendy-gwyn or Whitland, Dyfed) under the authority of

Hywel Dda, when the Laws were formulated. Not all the details given in the books can now be accepted as accurate. None of the extant manuscripts is a copy of any document which might have been formulated at Tŷ Gwyn, but it is accepted that they contain a nucleus of material compiled during the lifetime of Hywel Dda. The laws were administered throughout Wales until the sixteenth century when, having largely survived the Edwardian conquest of 1282, they were abolished by the Acts of Union. One of the most interesting examples of the native Welsh law is that dealing with *galanas* (meaning 'murder' or 'manslaughter'), which reflects the importance placed on the concept of kinship and blood ties to the seventh or ninth degree. The practice of partible inheritance or gavelkind was also an intrinsic element in the native laws.

## *Gruffudd ap Llywelyn*

The most successful of the native Welsh princes of the immediate pre-Norman era was Gruffudd ap Llywelyn, the son of Llywelyn ap Seisyll. From his initial seizure of power in Gwynedd in 1039 and his victory over a Mercian army in the same year, he became a dominating figure in Wales, gaining Deheubarth and, from 1055, holding the whole of Wales under his sway. It is thought that the devastation inflicted upon the English borderland (recorded in the Domesday Book in 1086) was the result of his efforts. His death at the hands of his own followers in 1063 deprived independent Wales of her most powerful ruler on the eve of the arrival of the Norman forces on the Anglo-Welsh border.

Thus the political fragmentation of Wales remained a reality throughout this period. Wales was a land of many kingdoms and many dynasties. Political unity was invariably transient and ephemeral, achieved by military might alone. The achievements of one generation were almost always undone in the next. 'They obstinately and proudly refuse to submit to one ruler' was the shrewd comment of Gerald of Wales at the end of the twelfth century.

## Early Welsh society

The Welsh had evolved a 'tribal' society in which blood relationships were all-important. This society was made up of bondsmen and free tribesmen who co-existed in a mixture of small nucleated and some scattered settlements called *maenors*, groups of which formed *cantrefs*, the basic units of royal administration. The bond population was concentrated in compact *maenors* in lowland areas which suited an agrarian economy, organized on manorial principles. In the upland areas free communities practised a pastoral economy and were grouped in more extensive *maenors*. Family relationships through the principle of kindred were well established, and circles of kindred to the fifth degree were recognized. These principles were to survive the coming of the Normans.

# 2

# From Norman Conquest
# to Edwardian Conquest

## *The Norman Conquest*

The Normans were one of Europe's most influential peoples in the early Middle Ages, enjoying an authority which ran from Sicily to Scotland. In September 1066, William of Normandy, accompanied by 5,000 Norman knights and a few thousand others, landed in southern England and launched what was to be the last major, successful invasion of the British Isles. At Pevensey in mid-October they swiftly defeated Harold's forces and rapidly brought the south-east of England under their control.

In order to realize his aim of setting up a strong centralized government, William allotted border territories to powerful followers on the Channel coast, the north of England and the border area between Wales and England. There was no Norman conquest of Wales as such; what occurred were isolated invasions by Norman lords who seized lands for themselves. Upon the Welsh border William established three earldoms – William FitzOsbern at Hereford, Roger of Montgomery at Shrewsbury and Hugh of Avranches at Chester. From each of these bases advances were made into Wales. Domesday Book shows clearly that much of the lands which had previously formed part of the Welsh kingdoms of Gwynedd and Powys now lay in Norman hands, although the area colonized was limited. Meanwhile, in the south, Gwent alone had been colonized by the year of the Conqueror's death in 1087. Domesday Book suggests that an agreement had been reached between William and Rhys ap Tewdwr, King of Deheubarth, that

Rhys should retain his authority in his own kingdom and perhaps in other parts of south Wales, especially Morgannwg and Brycheiniog, which lay outside Norman control.

The reign of William Rufus (1087–1100), who unsuccessfully invaded Wales on three separate occasions, witnessed some reversal in Norman fortunes in both north and south Wales amidst renewed conflict. But Rhys's death in 1093, opposing the Norman advance into Brycheiniog, rapidly led to the Norman conquest of almost the whole of south Wales. Further advances from border bases enabled Norman lords to found the major Marcher lordships of Cardigan, Pembroke, Brecon and Glamorgan. Thus the Norman 'conquest' of Wales was an extremely piecemeal affair with no centralized direction; no single, wholesale conquest was ever attempted.

### Motte-and-bailey castles

As the Norman magnates pressed forward into Wales from their border bases, they consolidated their position with castles, not massive, elaborate stone buildings, but earth and timber structures known as motte-and-bailey castles. The motte was the stronghold and consisted of a mound, usually some twenty to thirty feet in height, surrounded by wooden buildings within a palisade and defended all round by a moat, wet or dry, with its counterscarp. Adjoining the motte were one or more baileys, oval or right-angled enclosures with one gateway at the furthest point away from the motte, again defended by ditch and rampart. Access from bailey to motte was gained only by means of a sloping bridge across the ditch between the two. The original motte can still be clearly seen at Cardiff (now surrounded by a stone tower), while at Rhuddlan the Norman motte rises to the south-east of the Edwardian castle. Some motte-and-bailey castles were later rebuilt in stone, preserving the outlines of their motte-and-bailey origins. These include Cilgerran, Skenfrith, Tretower and Llawhaden.

It was this Norman advance which constituted the decisive stage in the creation of the March of Wales – that part of Wales which lay under the authority of the English Crown. In each lordship the Norman earl responsible for the conquest of the land assumed the extensive range of powers previously exercised in the same areas by the native Welsh kings. Indeed, the new lordships enjoyed practical independence of the English Crown; the Marcher lords retained their regalian rights and ruled like miniature kings. Royal interest and direction in Wales remained at best partial and spasmodic. The contrast between Norman England and Norman Wales is, therefore, striking. In England, the Normans inherited a kingdom where royal authority had already been centralized. In Wales this authority had remained dispersed among a number of rulers, a dispersal perpetuated by the Norman advance after which authority was vested in a mosaic of near-independent lordships.

## Gwynedd, Powys and Deheubarth

It is clear that there was an element of fluidity and fragility about the kingdoms of Wales in the eleventh century. Three or four stand out: Gwynedd, Powys, Deheubarth and perhaps Morgannwg. The period after 1093 saw the beginning in north Wales of a long period of conflict which led to the gradual recovery from Norman rule of much of the area, and the eventual re-establishment of Gwynedd and Powys as major political entities.

Gwynedd, under the rule of Gruffudd ap Cynan (d.1137) and his son Owain Gwynedd (d.1170), was provided with stable leadership over an extensive area which extended from the Dyfi to the Dee, and which enabled it to withstand two full-scale invasions by Henry II. The beneficiary of a secure geographical position and agricultural base, Gwynedd was uniquely well equipped to assume the leadership of the 'Welsh resurgence' of the twelfth and thirteenth centuries. Indeed, Owain Gwynedd threatened Powys by extending his dominion eastward into the buffer 'middle country' between the Conwy and the Dee.

But Powys too had prospered under a period of relative stability during the reign of Madog ap Maredudd (d. 1160) and had expanded eastwards beyond Offa's Dyke into lands which had previously been occupied by the Anglo-Saxons and the Normans.

Owain Gwynedd also challenged the Norman position in the south-west by annexing Ceredigion. But in this part of Wales it was Rhys ap Gruffydd (d. 1197) who wrested Ceredigion and most of Ystrad Tywi from Norman control, and thus restored much of south-west Wales to its ancient dynasty. Rhys's territory was not as extensive as the ancient kingdom of Deheubarth – the Normans were firmly in control of Pembroke and other lordships on the southern coastline – but it remained a considerable entity.

By the third quarter of the twelfth century, therefore, these three kingdoms represented a tangible sphere of native political influence, covering more than half the surface area of Wales, called *Wallia* or *Pura Wallia* which stood in clear contradistinction to the sphere of Norman influence called *Marchia Wallie*. The political geography of the kingdoms had achieved much fixity. The partitioning of their lands and the annexation of frontier areas did not undermine the general stability and cohesion which had been wrought. The concept that Wales was composed historically of three kingdoms ruled from the principal seats of Aberffraw in Gwynedd, Mathrafal in Powys and Dinefwr in Deheubarth became deeply ingrained and survived throughout the medieval period. It is evident that the rulers of these kingdoms attempted to establish a notion of kingship which combined traditional elements with the new feudal influences. Each ruler governed an independent kingdom, and did homage and fealty to the English monarchy in respect of his patrimony – a conscious effort to formalize the relationship between the rulers of Wales and the English Crown.

### Geoffrey of Monmouth

Born in *c.* 1090 in the vicinity of Monmouth town. Almost nothing is known of his early life. He may have served as a canon in the house of the Augustinian canons in St George's, Oxford. He was ordained priest in St Stephen's in February 1152 and was consecrated Bishop of St Asaph within a week. There is no evidence that he ever visited his see. He spent most of his life at Oxford where he died, probably in 1155. His early association with south-east Wales is reflected in his writings. His most important work is *Historia Regum*

*Britanniae* which appeared at the beginning of 1136 and which relates the 'history' of the Britons from the coming of Brutus to the arrival of the Saxons. Late in life he wrote his *Vita Merlini*, a Latin hexameter poem of 1,528 lines. The importance of the *Historia* lies in the credence given by generations of late medieval Welsh poets to its thesis that Brutus the Trojan, the supposed ancestor of the Welsh, had once ruled over a unified Britain; from this it was easy to deduce that a new Welsh leader had a moral right to the throne of Britain. This mythology was significant in Welsh support for Owain Glyndŵr and for Henry Tudor (Henry VII).

## Medieval social and economic life

The relative stability provided by these native rulers towards the end of the twelfth century enabled their kingdoms to experience some measure of recovery from the spoliation of the Norman period. An attempt was made to change the pattern of social organization in order to increase the resources of the native rulers' lands and to exploit more intensively their agrarian resources. In some areas the large number of bondsmen in the population was reorganized and moved in the hope that this would prove an incentive to the colonization of more marginal lands. The new terms of tenure were roughly equal to those granted to freemen. A second change was the settlement upon the soil of kindred groups of freemen in scattered sharelands. This eventually produced a dispersed settlement pattern, which stood in striking contrast to the clustered settlements of the bond communities. At the same time a small group of privileged free proprietors accumulated substantial estates and formed the nucleus of an official class of administrators required by the Welsh rulers.

Other social changes were also afoot. To consolidate their lands the Normans built castles of earth and timber (motte-and-bailey) at strategic points, the most important of which were later replaced by massive stone structures such as Brecon and Cardiff. Little walled towns were then built around the castles, and were peopled initially by Norman merchants, craftsmen and ex-soldiers who were granted trading and commercial rights and privileges. These were the first towns in Wales, bastide towns, small fortified settlements entirely alien to the Welsh. 'The Welsh have no towns' was Gerald of Wales's comment at the end of the twelfth century. A new agrarian economy based on the manor was also introduced by the Normans. The open-field system required land which was mainly low-lying with good soils, together with a moderate climate and rainfall, conditions found in eastern and south Wales, the very areas colonized by the Normans. Of some interest is the division of many Norman lordships into Englishries and Welshries. The former, the low-lying areas surrounding the castles and the boroughs, adopted the manorial system; the latter, on higher ground, retained their agrarian economy and native institutions though under Norman supervision. Large-scale farming and the growth of towns and trade in Wales were directly the result of the Norman conquest.

## The Church

As devoted Churchmen the Normans were determined to reform the religious life of Wales on the Continental pattern. The Welsh Church was largely robbed of its independence. In 768 the so-called 'Celtic Church' of the saints had agreed to conform with certain practices and customs of the Roman Church. These churches had come together to form individual bishoprics on the English pattern. There is no evidence of a superior Welsh archbishop, but equally there was no recognition of the superiority of the Archbishop of Canterbury. The *clas* organization of the Welsh Church was gradually replaced by Norman practices. The four territorial dioceses of Bangor, St Davids, Llandaff and St Asaph came into existence, and a parish structure was gradually set up. The Norman kings, and Henry I in particular, attempted to ensure that all bishops were political nominees, favourable to Norman rule, if not Normans themselves. All bishops were to be appointed by, and owed a profession of obedience to, the Archbishop of Canterbury.

## Early stone castles

Part of Chepstow Castle was the earliest stone building known in Wales, where, before 1071, William FitzOsbern had erected an oblong tower of two storeys made of stone. Generally the process of replacement in stone was gradual, continuous and piecemeal. The first stone castles 'grew' out of the old motte-and-bailey castles. Wales has the ruins of a number of twelfth-century keeps; Ogmore has a rectangular keep while Coity and Newcastle (both near Bridgend in Glamorgan) have square keeps. Dolwyddelan, built by one of the Welsh princes in the thirteenth century, has a striking rectangular keep and a stockade rebuilt in stone.

Free-standing circular keeps, more easily defensible, followed in the thirteenth century, and there are numerous examples in Dyfed, Powys and Gwent. The finest specimen in Wales is the 75-feet-high tower built c. 1200 by William Marshall within Pembroke Castle. The same technique is evident at Skenfrith and Caldicot in Gwent and Tretower and Bronllys in Powys. There is a striking round keep at Dolbadarn Castle and an unusual 'D'-shaped structure at Ewloe in Clwyd. probably built at the orders of Llywelyn ab Iorwerth, and proof enough of the mastery of the art of castle building by native Welsh rulers.

The implementation of these reforms was fraught with difficulties. Bernard, Bishop of St Davids from 1115 to 1148, claimed for himself the status of an archbishop, a claim which was revived by Gerald of Wales (who was part Norman and part Welsh) at the end of the twelfth century. Even greater resistance was forthcoming from Bangor, where there was no real bishop from 1092 to 1120. Gradually, however, the Norman influence won the day, and Norman nominees were enthroned at Llandaff in 1107, St Davids in 1115, Bangor in 1120 and St Asaph in 1143. The new bishops spared no effort to overhaul the organization of the Church and to eradicate surviving Celtic practices such as the marriage of the clergy. The appointment of archdeacons and deans was made on a large scale. Even now Welsh resistance was not at an end. The clergy of Bangor, acting under the protection of Owain Gwynedd in the 1160s, adamantly refused the demands of Thomas à Becket,

Archbishop of Canterbury, that their newly elected bishop should swear fealty to Canterbury.

### Gerald of Wales

Born in c. 1146 at Manorbier, Dyfed, a descendant of Rhys ap Tewdwr, Prince of Deheubarth. His father William de Barri was the lord of Manorbier. Gerald was very conscious of his mixed Welsh and Norman lineage. He was educated at the Church School in Gloucester and in Paris, where he mastered Latin styles of writing and became familiar with the 'authorities'. He returned to Wales in 1175, held a number of Church livings and became a zealous ecclesiastical reformer. He was nominated bishop of St Davids in 1176 and 1198, but was twice rejected by the king. He taught law in Paris, served as a royal clerk in Henry II's court from 1184 to 1194 and travelled widely, accompanying Prince John to Ireland in 1185 and Archbishop Baldwin through Wales in 1188. These journeys produced some of his most important writings including *The Story of the Journey through Wales* and *A Description of Wales*. In later life he pleaded passionately his right to be enthroned bishop of St Davids and visited Rome three times. He lost the fight and devoted the rest of his life to writing and editing. He died in 1223, and is noted as one of Wales's greatest writers in Latin.

Thus the Welsh evidence closely complements the general struggle of the time to make the Church independent of secular power. The same kind of secular involvement is evident in the story of the Cistercians, the last of the reforming orders, following the Benedictines and the Augustinians. The early Cistercian houses – Tintern (1131), Margam (1147) and Neath (1130) in the south and Basingwerk (1132) in the north – never won the hearts of the Welsh people. But the Abbey of Whitland (1140) and her 'daughters' and 'grand-daughters', founded from 1143 to 1201, really took root in Wales, many of them founded and all richly endowed by the native Welsh princes. Perhaps the most famous is Strata Florida, founded by a Norman in 1164 and re-established and richly endowed by the Lord Rhys in 1184. There was perhaps an inevitable cleavage between houses such as Margam and Tintern, established in the

March before 1150, and those founded under native patronage. Many of the Cistercian houses became keen supporters of the national aspirations and political endeavours of the Welsh rulers who had endowed them so handsomely.

## Llywelyn ab Iorwerth

The political map of Wales was simpler in the thirteenth century than in the twelfth, a simplification largely created by the dominance of the three great principalities of Gwynedd, Powys and Deheubarth, and above all by the sustained hegemony which Gwynedd came to secure. Following the death of the Lord Rhys in 1197, the history of Deheubarth degenerated into a recurrent and complex tangle of domestic squabbles. Northern Ceredigion was overrun by Llywelyn ab Iorwerth of Gwynedd in 1208, and from 1212 his power over Deheubarth was unchallenged, the kingdom's native rulers having become no more than 'puny chiefs'. Powys, now divided into two parts, and victim of the effects of partible inheritance, was perhaps the weakest of the Welsh kingdoms, and, after the crushing defeat of Gwenwynwyn, lord of southern Powys, by King John in 1208, could not hope to survive other than as a satellite of either the King of England or the Prince of Gwynedd. Indeed, in each of the three Welsh kingdoms, the death of the powerful rulers of the late twelfth century was followed by a contested succession, but, whereas in Deheubarth and Powys, the unity of the kingdoms was never restored, in Gwynedd the emergence to power at the end of the twelfth century of Llywelyn ab Iorwerth, a grandson of Owain Gwynedd, saw the uniting of the kingdom once more under the strong hand of a single ruler.

Llywelyn was determined to overcome his relatives to hold Gwynedd which he regarded as his rightful heritage. He enjoyed such a measure of success that by 1204 King John recognized him as lord of Gwynedd and gave him his illegitimate daughter Joan in marriage. In 1208 Llywelyn revealed the extent of his ambitions when he annexed southern Powys and marched into Ceredigion.

But he was growing too powerful for John's liking, and his aggression against neighbouring territories had incurred resistance within Wales. This resistance John turned to his advantage in 1211 when, having led two devastatingly successful campaigns into north Wales, he compelled Llywelyn to agree to the most humiliating terms.

Llywelyn, however, was soon able to take advantage of a general Welsh resistance to John's measures for the permanent conquest of the country and headed a sustained campaign now supported by his former adversaries. The common Welsh front both thwarted John's ambitions and enabled Llywelyn to achieve a dominant position among the Welsh princes, a position which seemed to augur well for the creation of a Welsh polity whereby the other princes would be tied by bonds of homage and fealty to him.

### The royal line of Gwynedd (simplified)

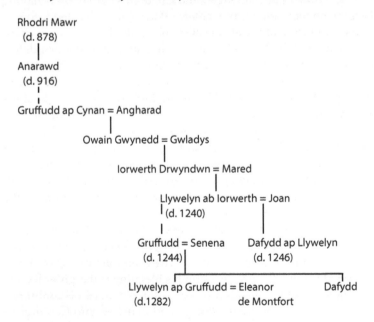

For the rest of his life he exerted a powerful influence over his fellow princes and thus reduced the involvement of the English Crown in the affairs of Wales, but he never achieved formal royal recognition of his territorial and theoretical achievements. Yet these achievements were real. In 1216 he summoned the Welsh princes to a kind of national parliament at Aberdyfi and divided Deheubarth among the descendants of the Lord Rhys, an arrangement which prevailed for a quarter of a century. At Worcester in 1218 he met the new boy king Henry III to whom he performed homage followed by the other Welsh princes, while the English government was forced to acknowledge his pre-eminence.

Llywelyn's main concern during his last years was the prevention of the fragmentation of his extensive domain upon his death. In October 1238 he again summoned all the Welsh princes to a council at Strata Florida Abbey, where each swore loyalty to Dafydd, Llywelyn's son by Joan. Llywelyn was anxious that Dafydd alone should be designated as his heir in preference to his elder but illegitimate son Gruffudd, and looked to the English monarchy to ensure an unchallenged succession. Content with the more local title of 'Prince of Aberffraw and Lord of Snowdon' rather than the more prestigious 'Prince of Wales', Llywelyn had, both theoretically and in practical terms, assembled all the ingredients to justify the use of the latter title. As he lay dying at Aberconwy in April 1240, his main preoccupation must have been Dafydd's succession.

## Dafydd ap Llywelyn

Llywelyn's fears soon proved justified. Henry III, far from intervening to ensure a smooth succession in Dafydd's favour, took advantage of the dissension between Dafydd and Gruffudd and of the disparate ambitions of the other Welsh princes, to confine Dafydd's power to Gwynedd alone. In 1244, Gruffudd was killed while attempting to escape from the Tower of London where he had been held prisoner by the King. Two years later Dafydd, engaged in a desperate but promising attempt to increase his realms, died suddenly without heir. In April 1247 Owain and Llywelyn, the two eldest sons of Gruffudd, were forced to agree to the Peace of Woodstock. Gwynedd was divided: Henry III took the east and Llywelyn and Owain the west. The prospect of even further division to provide for two younger brothers was envisaged. The other Welsh rulers were to render their homage directly to the King rather than through the Prince of Gwynedd. Moreover, the King had established himself on a ring of strategic points – Montgomery, Builth, Carmarthen and Cardigan. The future looked bleak, and the efforts of Llywelyn to create a united, independent state seemed in vain.

## *Llywelyn ap Gruffudd*

Eight years of relative peace came to an end in 1254 when Prince Edward (later Edward I) was given charge of all the Crown lands in Wales. In the following year Llywelyn ap Gruffudd imprisoned his brothers, whom he had defeated at the Battle of Bryn Derwin, and took west Gwynedd for himself. In a series of dramatically successful campaigns from 1255 to 1258 he regained east Gwynedd, conquered Meirionnydd, Builth, Deheubarth and Powys, and raided deep into Pembroke and Glamorgan. He then assumed the symbolically significant style of 'Prince of Wales', gathered together the lesser princes and received their homage. He was well placed to take advantage of Henry III's quarrel with the English barons. Indeed, in June 1265 Llywelyn made a formal alliance at Pipton with Simon de Montfort, a bargain sealed by his betrothal to Simon's daughter Eleanor. Although only seven weeks later Simon was defeated and killed at the Battle of Evesham, the royalist resurgence did not deter Llywelyn. His hegemony was formally acknowledged by Henry III in September 1267 by the Treaty of Montgomery, when the style 'Prince of Wales' was accepted, as was his right to the homage and fealty of the Welsh lords. He alone was to pay tribute and perform homage to the English king, and he was granted the extensive tracts of land which he had won on the borders.

Llywelyn had thus created a Principality of Wales composed of the three twelfth-century kingdoms of Gwynedd, Powys and Deheubarth as well as parts of the March. This was not the result of military might, of conquest, as such, but was rather the culmination of an internal political evolution. This creation of a feudal polity within Wales was a dramatic reversal of a situation, deeply ingrained, whereby the lands of Welsh rulers were held as fiefs directly from the king of England. Llywelyn had thus surpassed even the

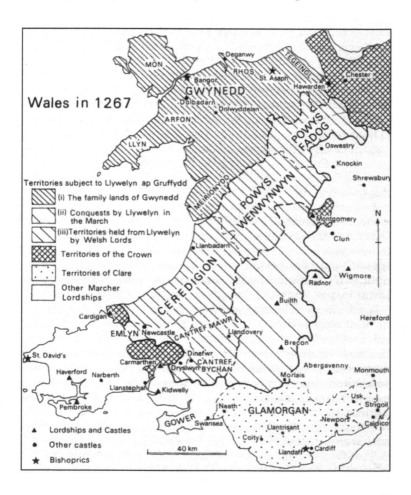

Wales in 1267

Territories subject to Llywelyn ap Gruffydd

(i) The family lands of Gwynedd

(ii) Conquests by Llywelyn in the March

(iii) Territories held from Llywelyn by Welsh Lords

Territories of the Crown

Territories of Clare

Other Marcher Lordships

▲ Lordships and Castles

● Other castles

★ Bishoprics

achievements of his grandfather, whose stone-built castles at Ewloe, Dolwyddelan, Dolbadarn, Cricieth and Bere he improved. But the opportunity to consolidate the government and defence of his lands proved to be brief indeed.

## Government and society under the Welsh princes

The strong central authority which had been built up perhaps inevitably brought about novel departures in the field of government. The two Llywelyns presided over a council of officials, vassal lords and ecclesiastics (rather like the English *parliamenta* of the age) which co-ordinated the administrative and judicial functions of this miniature feudal state, and built up a class of civil servants (such as Ednyfed Fychan and later his two sons Goronwy and Tudur) who helped them to govern and to tax their subjects. The work of a reformed and sometimes oppressive body of officials in the commotes was supervised by a central bureaucracy which included a treasurer and a chancellor in charge of a great seal and a privy seal.

The substructure of tribal society was challenged by far-reaching changes in traditional law and custom. A legal renaissance led to the revision of legal texts which reflected the new quasi-feudal trends. These trends were also reflected in the way in which the formal personal obligations and homage traditionally owed to a Welsh leader were now being replaced by the duties of landholding and feudal homage. The penal system was being reformed, and there was a tendency to stress the responsibility of the individual rather than of the kindred. Not that the kindred principle disappeared; the principle of inheritance was based on knowledge of kindred, while oaths had to be supported by oath-helpers in personal actions. These were drawn from circles of kindred to the fifth degree.

There were parallel changes in economic organization – the growth of town life and the spread of a money economy. Small market towns were founded on the estates of the Welsh princes and lords. Trade by sea and by land was initiated, notably the cattle trade with England. The growth of a cash economy was a marked feature: Llywelyn was able to impose a general tax on movables and, in the rural areas surrounding the towns, to change payment of tribute in kind into cash rents. These changing economic circumstances somewhat undermined clan co-operation, strengthened the sense of individual proprietorship and underlined the link between the state and the individual. On the other hand, the efforts of the two Llywelyns as state-builders, flouting local sentiment and tribal feeling, and the growth of a more modern consciousness of Welsh nationhood (then dawning at the court of Aberffraw) were stunted by clan loyalties, the prevalence of localism and conservative traditions, and in the long term attracted hostility in certain quarters in Wales. Finally, a more permanent and stable agricultural settlement was taking the place of the free movement of the old warrior class. By the end of the thirteenth century, much of Wales was dotted with small hamlets which rather resembled English villages of the period. Yet, again, the arable fields linked to the hamlets were arranged on a communal basis reflecting the traditional tribal practices of the people. The old survived with the new.

## The war of 1277

In 1272 Henry III was succeeded by Edward I, a capable military tactician and statesman. It became his ambition to make Britain a united kingdom through the conquest of Wales and Scotland. It would appear moreover that Llywelyn deliberately antagonized Edward. He failed to attend his coronation in August 1274, he ceased to pay the customary tribute which he owed, and on five separate occasions between November 1274 and April 1276 he refused to perform homage to Edward. He determined to marry Eleanor, the daughter of the dead Simon de Montfort, the leader of the baronial opposition against Henry III, thus reviving memories of the baronial struggle against the Crown. At the very time that relations between

English king and Welsh prince were dramatically deteriorating, Llywelyn faced trouble within Wales. The princes of south-west Wales rebelled against him, and he faced the enmity of the barons of the March. He lost both the south-west and large areas of the March during the winter of 1276–7, and in the following July Edward led a strong army along the coast from Chester. He made good progress, established strong points at Flint, Rhuddlan and Degannwy, and sent his fleet to cut off Anglesey and its corn supplies. Llywelyn, faced by the threat of famine and winter, felt compelled to seek terms.

The Treaty of Aberconwy of November 1277 brought an end to the conflict, but its terms were predictably humiliating for Llywelyn. He was deprived of all his lands except Gwynedd west of the River Conwy, a return to the territorial position of 1247, while almost all the Welsh princes were to do homage direct to Edward. His retention of the title Prince of Wales was meaningless and a mockery. Before the end of the year Llywelyn went to London to do homage to Edward. Now the power of the Crown in Wales was very much stronger. Large tracts of land in Cardigan and Carmarthen lay in royal hands, and royal castles such as Builth, Aberystwyth, Flint and Rhuddlan were built to surround what remained of Llywelyn's domain.

## The war of 1282

Relations between Llywelyn and Edward were reasonably friendly for four years. The English King permitted, attended and paid for the marriage of Llywelyn and Eleanor in 1278. Three years later Edward's insistence that a dispute between Llywelyn and Gruffydd ap Gwenwynwyn of Powys should be tried by English law poisoned relations. There was much indignation in east Gwynedd and Ceredigion that the King's officials were acting oppressively against the native Welsh. Dafydd, Llywelyn's brother, began the war when he attacked the castle of Hawarden in March 1282, an attack which quickly led to revolts breaking out all over Wales. Llywelyn had little choice but to join in what would inevitably develop into a fight to the finish.

Initially Edward met with severe reverses – his troops based on Carmarthen were defeated at Llandeilo and his sea-borne force from Anglesey was annihilated as it tried to cross the Menai Straits – and he made offers of peace by which Llywelyn would have lost almost everything. But the Welsh Prince was determined to press on.

In November, perhaps lured by false promises of support, he hastened to central Wales, his weakest point, and launched an attack on Builth Castle. A battle at Irfon Bridge ensued on 11 December during which Llywelyn was killed by Stephen de Frankton, an English horseman. His head was cut off and sent to Edward at Rhuddlan. Although Dafydd struggled on until the following June, he too was finally betrayed to the English and met a cruel death at Shrewsbury. Welsh independence was finally at an end. From this time on, Wales was to be an integral, if troublesome, part of the realm of England.

# 3

# From Conquest to Union

## *The Edwardian settlement*

After the death of the native princes of Gwynedd Edward's role in Wales was that of the all-powerful conqueror. He journeyed through Wales in an attempt to underline the military might of England and, like William the Conqueror before him, he ventured as far as St David's. In the Statute of Rhuddlan, or Statute of Wales, of 1284, Edward established the principles for the government of his recent conquests.

Not that the Statute applied to the whole of Wales; the fundamental division between Principality and March remained throughout the later Middle Ages. Edward was in no position to attempt to annex the March to his realms. On the contrary, he created a number of new independent Marcher lordships in north-east Wales, previously the Perfeddwlad, Gwynedd to the east of the River Conwy – Denbigh, Ruthin, Bromfield and Yale, and Chirk – as lavish and handsome rewards for the barons who had aided him in the conquest of Wales, and thus created a new Marcher aristocracy to be largely entrusted with the pacification and settlement of Wales. A relatively small part of Wales remained in the hands of the Crown. By the Statute of Rhuddlan, Snowdonia was divided into the counties of Anglesey, Caernarfon and Merioneth, to be under the authority of a new official, the Justice of North Wales, with his administrative capital at Caernarfon. Out of the *cantref* of Englefield was formed the county of Flint which was placed under the rule of the Justice of Chester. A Justice of South Wales, who governed the existing counties of Carmarthen and Cardigan, had held office since 1280. There was no kind of administrative or constitutional unity in the government of the Crown lands in Wales in the later Middle Ages.

The Statute of 1284 further reflects the fact that Edward reigned in an age of exceptional legal renaissance. Each of the new shires was placed under a sheriff, an officer new to Wales, and a system of courts was established on the English pattern – the sessions, held

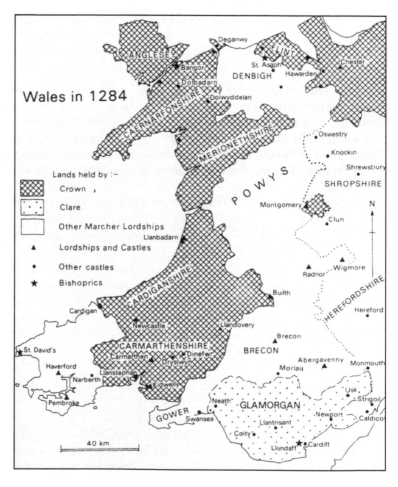

by the justice, the county court, the sheriff's turn, and the hundred or commote courts, presided over by the sheriff. The Statute outlined in detail the writs which would be available in the new network of courts. English criminal law was to be used, but native Welsh law was to be retained in some civil actions and particularly in certain aspects of land law. No change was made in the crucial area of inheritance; partible succession remained the order of the day. The Statute was not an uncompromisingly harsh document; it contained an element of conciliation, and some Welshmen of the fourteenth century regarded it as a charter which protected the rights and privileges of the Welsh. The Welsh counties remained outside the jurisdiction of the central courts of Westminster and did not elect representatives to Parliament. Overall, the Edwardian settlement of Wales was thoroughly single-minded and possessed coherence.

## Thirteenth-century castles

The main development in the thirteenth century was the bailey or curtain wall together with the adoption of the rounded mural or flanking tower. These wall towers provided a series of self-contained strongholds at a number of separate points along the curtain wall. Some such towers were semicircular and solid; others were hollow, providing extra accommodation. Rounded wall towers are visible at Chepstow, built by William Marshall, at Cilgerran, built by Marshall's son, and at Grosmont and Skenfrith, reconstructed by the Justiciar Hubert de Burgh. Increasingly powerful gatehouses consisting of twin towers on either side were often added. An early gatehouse still stands at White Castle in Gwent, and a partly ruined one at Montgomery. That at Cricieth was probably added by Edward I.

The pinnacle of achievement was reached with the development of the concentric castle (provided with two complete sets of defences) in the late thirteenth century. Caerphilly, covering fully twenty-five acres and second only to Dover in its size, was built by a Marcher lord, as indeed was Kidwelly, overlooking the River Gwendraeth. The castles built by Edward I mark the climax. Of the four built after the war of 1277, perhaps the most outstanding feature is the great round tower at Flint Castle known as the 'donjon' and possibly intended as a residence for the royal Justice of Chester. The post-1282 castles, one of the most remarkable groups of medieval monuments to be seen anywhere in Europe, have been discussed in the text. Investment in these castles amounted to the modern equivalent of about £50 million at a time when the population of England and Wales was about one-twentieth of its present level. Raglan Castle was built by Sir William ap Thomas between about 1430 and 1445 after the Glyndŵr rebellion.

## The castles and the boroughs

To provide for the security of his conquests Edward embarked upon an ambitious and far-reaching programme of castle-building, already initiated at four strategic sites after the war of 1277 and extended and intensified from June 1282. Hope was soon repaired. Ruthin, Denbigh and Holt were under construction by Edward's barons by the autumn of the same year. By the summer of 1283 work had begun on the three great new castles of Conwy, Harlech and Caernarfon. The resources expended on this work were immense: stone, lead, iron and steel, rope and timber were commandeered from all parts of Edward's realms; manpower was assembled amazingly quickly on a remarkable scale; the best master-craftsmen available were hired to supervise and coordinate the work. Master James of St George, a military architect of genius and a skilful administrator who had major building experience in Savoy to his credit, master-minded the basic design of all the great Edwardian castles in Wales. Extraordinary industry characterized the construction; the whole of Conwy and most of Caernarfon were completed by the end of 1287 and Harlech by 1289. No expense was spared; by 1301 some £80,000 had been expended by Edward on his eight major new castles in Wales. This massive investment has been compared with the resources required to assemble a fleet of nuclear submarines today, and it has been claimed that Edward I never succeeded in conquering Scotland because of the immense resources expended in securing the conquest of Wales. The Welsh castles were an intrinsic part of a coherent strategy for the subjugation of native Wales, and bear testimony to the ruthless energy and fierce determination of Edward's personality. Architecturally, they combined a dramatic sense of power with great beauty of form. Primarily instruments of military domination, they were also the seats of civilian governance and the headquarters of a new administrative regime. The quasi-imperial character of Edward's vision of his conquest of Wales was most clearly demonstrated at Caernarfon Castle, the administrative capital of the new province of north Wales, with its polygonal towers and bands of contrasting coloured stone in conscious emulation of the Theodosian wall of Constantinople, a structure without parallel in the whole of western Europe.

Together with the castles came the boroughs, established by Edward in the wake of his victories over the Welsh – Flint, Aberystwyth and Rhuddlan in 1277, Caernarfon, Conwy, Harlech, Cricieth and Bere in 1282–3, Beaumaris in 1295. Major new boroughs were also established by Edward's barons at centres such as Holt, Denbigh, Ruthin and Overton. Peopled by a privileged English, and hence alien, burgess class, these new towns transformed the pattern of economic life of native Wales. Welshmen were prohibited from inhabiting the towns and from trading or carrying arms within their walls. A classic colonial situation was thus deliberately created, designed to keep vigorously alive the spirit of conquest and of racial cleavage and superiority. Small wonder that the boroughs and their alien and privileged burgesses were to become the most consistent target of Welsh resentment in the fourteenth century.

## Crown and community

Fourteenth-century Wales generally enjoyed an unprecedented period of peace, security, prosperity and confidence. Welsh reactions to the reality of English rule in the fourteenth century were disparate and inconsistent. Certainly, within many Marcher communities large numbers of native Welshmen held official positions, a practice encouraged by some lords as the most effective means of securing stable government. The same trend was evident to some extent within the former principality of Llywelyn. Even before the conquest a significant element in the Welsh *uchelwyr* class, or aristocracy, had been won over to the patronage of the English Crown, and after 1282 many of these and some former supporters of Llywelyn displayed an embarrassing haste to win the favour of the new regime. Edward I could rely upon the services of a number of prominent figures in Gwynedd, thus establishing a rapport which transcended even Madog ap Llywelyn's rebellion in Anglesey in 1294.

When the government of the Principality of Wales was transferred by Edward to his son – the future Edward II – in 1301, the young prince inherited too the loyalty of a devoted group of servants of Welsh extraction who served him unflinchingly throughout the whole of his troubled reign. Soon after the Prince's accession in 1307 a host of difficulties faced him: the lords of the kingdom, some of them landowners in the March of Wales, formed leagues in opposition to the King, and in Glamorgan in 1316 Llywelyn Bren, lord of Senghennydd, rebelled against him. Yet the *uchelwyr* of Gwynedd, resisting the temptation to profit from the weakness of the English monarchy, remained loyal. Servants such as Sir Gruffudd Llwyd, a descendant of Ednyfed Fychan, steward to Llywelyn ab Iorwerth, and Rhys ap Gruffudd rendered powerful service and warm attachment to Edward and the Angevin cause during the last fateful months of his reign.

Although Edward III was uncertain of the attitude of the Welsh during the early years of his reign, the outbreak of the wars with France saw large numbers of prominent Welshmen serve in the English ranks. The poetry of Iolo Goch yields a vivid picture of the military achievements of Welshmen in France and lavishes praise on the English king. Similar indications of reconciliation between Welshmen and conqueror are evident in civilian life. Native officials generally acted as administrators at the commote level and participated in the work of the county and baronial courts. Some even became stewards and sheriffs. Regular requests for the advantage of English land and inheritance laws were made, and rapport between Crown and community was a prominent theme.

*Caernarfon Castle, Gwynedd, one of the masterpieces of concentric castle-building undertaken by Edward I after his conquest of Wales in 1282.*

## Discord and rebellion

Yet alongside the tradition of reconciliation and peaceful coexistence, there was inevitable hostility to the English regime, hostility stemming from racial pride and material discomfort arising out of the changing order of society. From time to time rebellions did occur in post-Conquest Wales. The first was led in 1286–7 by Rhys ap Maredudd, lord of Ystrad Tywi, a former ally of Edward I who had assisted him militarily during the Conquest but felt that he had been shabbily treated. His rising was quickly put down; it was no more than the protest of a discontented individual who failed to win support outside south-west Wales and could not even command the loyalty of his own men.

Seven years later the rebellion of Madog ap Llywelyn in Anglesey was a very different affair. A descendant of the lords of Meirionnydd, Madog raised a revolt in 1294–5 which had dramatic repercussions in almost the whole of Wales, the royal lands in the north and south,

43

new and old Marcher lordships alike. In particular, in the south-east another disinherited local princeling, Morgan ap Maredudd, took the lead, and other local leaders, descended from the ancient Welsh dynasties, also emerged in Brecon and Cardiganshire. A classic anti-colonial rebellion, it was fuelled by deep resentment against alien rule and corrupt and arrogant royal and Marcher officialdom. Economic and social discontent had merged with aristocratic dissatisfaction and popular protest. The ingredients of a potentially successful national rebellion all coalesced. Madog even styled himself 'Prince of Wales'. Edward's response was speedy, thorough and successful. The Welsh lacked both the resources and the will to sustain such a rebellion.

The legacy of Madog's rebellion was considerable. Edward imposed heavy fines on Welsh communities, and in 1295 intensive work began on yet another massive stone castle at Beaumaris, soon to be surrounded by an alien borough. Moreover, harsh supplementary ordinances were issued by the King in the wake of the revolt: Welshmen were largely prevented from buying and selling land, carrying weapons, holding land or living within the boroughs, conducting business or meeting in groups. Thus the conciliatory tone of the Statute of 1284 was modified considerably by the punitive ordinances enacted in 1295.

The same combination of aristocratic discontent and economic distress fuelled the revolt of Llywelyn Bren, lord of Senghennydd in Glamorgan, in 1316. Harvest failure in 1314–15 and resultant plague account for the support rendered to Llywelyn. Yet again two royal armies crushed a rebellion which had devastated the whole of Glamorgan.

By the 1340s outbreaks of sporadic violence were occurring in north Wales. On St Valentine's Day 1345 Henry de Shaldeford, a burgess of Caernarfon and the Black Prince's attorney in north Wales, was murdered by an armed band of eighty men, led by Tudur and Hywel ap Goronwy, as he travelled from Denbigh to Caernarfon. The rift between the alien burgesses of towns such as Rhuddlan and Denbigh and the native Welsh was wide indeed, and fears were expressed that the very foundations of the Conquest lay in grave jeopardy. Racial tension, increased by the enforcement of administrative and fiscal reforms, lay near the surface in late medieval Wales. Yet large numbers of Welshmen readily served in the English armies in the war against France.

One famous and colourful Welshman who fought in the armies of the French, not the English, was Owain Lawgoch, great-nephew to Llywelyn ap Gruffudd. Owain issued a proclamation threatening to invade Wales and even set sail from France, but never reached Welsh shores. He was hailed by Welsh poets such as Gruffudd ap Maredudd as a potential deliverer of the Welsh. Thus rebellions in fourteenth-century Wales were rooted in personal protest, social unrest, racial tension and popular prophecy. Each of these elements was to come together in the rebellion of Owain Glyndŵr in 1400.

### Owain Lawgoch (Red-hand)

Born Owain ap Thomas ap Rhodri in *c.* 1330, a descendant of Llywelyn ab Iorwerth and a grandson of a brother of Llywelyn ap Gruffudd. He served in the armies of the King of France and enjoyed a distinguished career leading French mercenary forces against the English Crown. He was very conscious of the Welsh origins and ancestral rights of his family and came to Wales in 1363 to claim a patrimony in Montgomeryshire. He was proclaimed Prince of Wales by propagandists in the county. Following the defeat of an English fleet off La Rochelle in 1372, he was permitted by the French King to detach a naval force from Harfleur to conquer Wales, but was recalled by his master once he had taken Guernsey. A Scottish traitor by the name of John Lamb was hired by the English Crown to win his trust and murder him during the siege of Montagne-sur-Mer in July 1378. There are many references to him in Welsh prophetic poetry where he is often confused with Arthur. He was buried at the church of St Léger, four miles from the scene of his death.

## The Black Death of the fourteenth century

The society and economy of fourteenth-century Wales, and indeed of western Europe, were the inevitable victims of war, famine and plague. Apart from the rebellions of the immediate post-Conquest period and the revolt of Llywelyn Bren in 1316, Wales did not experience the ravages of war, and both Wales and England were relatively peaceful nations, avoiding the French experience of the savage battles of the Hundred Years' War which witnessed widespread pillaging by soldiers. The history of the Welsh Church in the early fourteenth century reflects an era of material reconsolidation, a trend encouraged and indeed assisted by the English Crown.

### Bishops' palaces

The bishops of St Davids were among the wealthiest landowners in medieval Wales, owning rich and substantial estates. There remains an outstanding group of medieval buildings at St David's: the ruins of the medieval precinct walls with the twin-towered Porth y Tŵr dating from c. 1300, the exquisite cathedral church, the fourteenth-century college of St Mary and the Bishop's Palace itself, the handiwork of a succession of distinguished builder-bishops. Three miles to the east of Pembroke is the bishop's residence at Lamphey comprising early thirteenth-century buildings: a hall, service rooms and a 'camera' or private apartment. The major episcopal residence at Llawhaden is a castle rather than a palace. The original castle was destroyed by the Welsh in 1192 and reconstructed at the beginning of the fourteenth century. It was used by the bishops down to the Reformation when it was largely abandoned in favour of the bishop's palace at Abergwili near Carmarthen.

But Wales could not escape the devastating impact of famine and plague. We have seen the effect of famine and the chronic shortage of food upon the population of Glamorgan in 1316. Perhaps its most significant effect was to weaken and hence reduce the resistance of the population to disease. In 1348 the advent of plague severely undermined the population growth and economic evolution of much of western Europe. Wales experienced its first lethal visitation during the winter of 1348–9, and plague spread rapidly from the south-east to the north-west and north-east. It proved to be the first of a series of devastating outbreaks of the Black Death. There were further serious eruptions in 1361, 1369, 1371 and 1393.

Although not all parts of Wales suffered to the same extent, the primary effect of the Black Death was to reduce substantially the size of the population, and, eventually, to bring about changes in landholding and economic transactions. Land was all too often left uncultivated, the bondsmen and their overseers dead or escaped in order to avoid rents and taxes. Both famine and plague were natural phenomena, but man cannot escape some share of blame for the social and economic crisis of the fourteenth century. This period saw the growth of ever more powerful lordships in the March of Wales and of a tendency to enforce harshly the rights and authority of the lords. During the century many lords, including the Crown, increasingly considered their lordships as sources of revenue to be exploited and squeezed oppressively, one reason for the widespread support so readily given to Owain Glyndŵr. A particular grievance existed in Wales because many of the survivors of the Black Death, unable to pay the dues expected of them as a group, were deprived of their lands by royal officials.

There was thus widespread resentment that king and lords alike, in an attempt to sustain the level of their income artificially, were taking unreasonable advantage of the aftermath of natural calamities. At the same time, many individuals did succeed in increasing their lands and in advancing socially. Estates began to be built up, and even the lower orders of society, now experiencing greater mobility, could enjoy economic and social prosperity, a theme prominent in fourteenth-century Welsh poetry.

## Owain Glyndŵr

Social tension and friction increased still more after about 1370: economic and social dislocation, seigneurial greed and pressure, political malaise and external threats were all reflected in a native restlessness. Difficulties were compounded by dramatic changes of personnel in the Marcher lordships in the late 1390s, changes brought about by the deaths or exile of a number of lords and their replacement by the favoured nominees of Richard II, all of which undermined and severed the crucial pattern of patronage and reward.

Richard himself was soon swept from power. On 16 September 1400 Owain Glyndŵr, lord of Glyndyfrdwy (a small village in the valley of the Dee between Corwen and Llangollen), who could claim descent from the royal lines of both Powys and Deheubarth, was proclaimed Prince of Wales by a small group of his family and friends. They then raided a number of the English boroughs of north-east Wales and other towns: Ruthin, Denbigh, Rhuddlan, Flint, Hawarden and Oswestry. They were soon overpowered and scattered; Henry IV led a short, punitive expedition into north Wales in October. It seemed a purely local affair: Reginald de Grey, lord of Ruthin, had seized part of Glyndŵr's lands and had accused him of treachery to the Crown. The rebellion was Glyndŵr's response. But the government responded unwisely: large subsidies were demanded from the Welsh population, and in 1401 penal legislation was passed which prohibited the Welsh from acquiring land in England or in the English towns in Wales and from being enrolled as burgesses, while the English were protected from conviction at the suit of Welshmen in Wales.

The Welsh reaction was swift. Conwy Castle was seized at Easter 1401 and held for two months, while Glyndŵr himself won much of north-west Wales, threatening Harlech and Caernarfon Castles. He sought help from the King of Scotland and the native Irish lords in response to a further expedition led by Henry IV in October. During 1402, Glyndŵr not only captured two leading English notables – Reginald de Grey of Ruthin and Edmund Mortimer – but also extended his activities to Gwent and Glamorgan, and evaded yet a third royal expedition. The course of 1403 saw Glyndŵr win over much of south-west Wales, join forces with Henry Percy (Hotspur) – who was killed by Henry's forces at Shrewsbury – and receive military assistance from French and Breton forces. The pinnacle of his ambitions was reached in 1404 when he captured the castles at Harlech, Aberystwyth and perhaps Cardiff. Even more significantly, he summoned a 'parliament' at Machynlleth, was crowned Prince of Wales before the envoys of France, Scotland and

Castile, devised his own great and privy seals and adopted the coat of arms of the princes of Gwynedd, signed a formal alliance with the French and received recognition of his position from the Bishops of Bangor and St Asaph.

Ambition, however, was beginning to cloud prudence and caution. In 1405 Glyndŵr concluded a wildly unrealistic Tripartite Indenture with the Earl of Northumberland and young Edmund Mortimer, whereby they resolved to dethrone Henry and to divide the whole of England and Wales between them. But a number of military defeats ensued in south-east Wales and in Anglesey and some former supporters began to submit to the King, a trend which rapidly gathered momentum in 1406. Glyndŵr and his followers now drafted a radical ecclesiastical programme, known as the Pennal policy, to make the Welsh Church independent of Canterbury and set up two universities in Wales to train native civil servants and clergymen. But the initiative was never regained. The French alliance collapsed in 1407, opposition to Henry IV was on the wane in England, and in 1408 even Harlech and Aberystwyth were recaptured by vigorous English armies. By 1410 the rebellion had simply petered out, though Glyndŵr himself remained uncaptured. His ultimate fate remains unknown, though his death has been placed in about 1416. He had shown himself to be a talented military tactician and a far-sighted political analyst, who commanded a quite remarkable measure of general support, extending widely both socially and geographically throughout Wales. His revolt was the last sustained protest by the native Welsh against the experience of conquest more than a century earlier.

Even greater humiliation lay in store for the Welsh upon the restoration of Lancastrian government to Wales. Predictably, the lands of the rebels were seized by the King, and severe fines were imposed upon an already impoverished people. The discriminatory legislation of 1401–2 greatly limited the freedom of the Welsh to hold office, to acquire lands or to achieve equality in law, yielding a profound sense of national grievance, and reducing the Welsh to the status of second-class citizens. True, in practice much of this legislation was overlooked or ignored, but it remained on the statute book to embarrass Welshmen and to restrict their ambitions and aspirations. The existence of the penal legislation explains the petitions which came from fifteenth-century Wales to be 'made English'. In 1439 William Gruffudd petitioned Parliament to be 'made English' to enable him to purchase and hold land according to English law and to 'enjoy all other liberties as other loyal Englishmen'. The restrictions on transmitting property to a single heir, on the buying and selling of land (in order to accumulate substantial estates), and on office-holding were especially keenly felt by the ambitious, socially mobile, emergent gentry class which prospered in the fifteenth century.

During the last years of his reign, between 1504 and 1507, Henry VII granted charters of privilege to his Principality of North Wales and to the north-eastern lordships created after the Conquest, charters intended to remove the restrictions imposed by the Lancastrian penal code. The inhabitants of these regions were in this way allowed to buy and sell land freely, to hold office in England and in the English boroughs in Wales, they were frequently released from burdensome archaic financial payments, and they were permitted to bequeath land by the custom of inheritance by the eldest son alone. These charters extended the privileges already conceded to many individuals by the grant of denizen status.

## Social and economic life in the fifteenth century

Generally this was an age of recovery from the baneful effects of rebellion: depopulation, agricultural depression and widespread devastation, all inevitable consequences of the guerrilla warfare practised by King and rebels alike – the burning of crops, the destruction of property, the pillaging of towns, these latter being seen as symbols of the excessive authority of king and lords Marcher. In general, seigneurial income in the fifteenth century never attained the high levels of much of the fourteenth. Yet for some elements in society the ingredients of a new-found prosperity existed. Much poor and marginal land, previously cultivated by an over-large population, went out of use. More land of better quality was available to be taken up by would-be purchasers and lessees. In an age when labour was in short supply, even the labourers found that they could command relatively high wages. The more fortunate of the gentry and the better-off tenants were the major beneficiaries of these changes. The cattle trade and the woollen and cloth trade flourished, which brought prosperity to some of the towns of the southern coast and the eastern border. The poetry of the period provides evidence of generous patronage, lavish hospitality and an abundance of high living. The religious life of the time reveals similar prosperity; there was widespread rebuilding, refurbishing and beautifying of parish churches all over Wales, even in poor rural areas, often facilitated by generous contributions from parishioners.

## Dafydd ap Gwilym

Born in c. 1320, reputedly in the parish of Llanbadarn Fawr in Dyfed, he was the most distinguished of the medieval Welsh poets, who brought innovations to the language, subject matter and metrical techniques of poetry. His family included several officials who held high office under the Crown in south-west Wales, among them his uncle and mentor, Llywelyn ap Gwilym (d. c. 1346), who served as Constable of Newcastle Emlyn. Dafydd's rich vocabulary reflects a wide knowledge of the Welsh poetry of previous centuries and a command of words of French origin. His personal pursuit of love is the primary theme of his verse, often associated with a forest setting of animals and birds. The novel cywydd verse form (seven-syllabled lines in rhyming couplets) became in his hands a highly flexible medium, sometimes interspersed with passages of racy, colloquial dialogue. He also made some use of the older Welsh bardic metres over which he displayed an equal mastery. Very little is known of his personal life. He evidently travelled widely throughout Wales and was acquainted with many contemporary poets. He died in c. 1370 and may be buried within the precincts of the monastery of Strata Florida in Dyfed. His reputed places of birth and burial are both now marked by commemorative plaques.

Above all, the disintegration of manorial and native economic institutions was accelerated by the upheavals of the Glyndŵr

*The Parliament House at Machynlleth, Powys, the meeting-place of the 'parliament' for Wales summoned in 1404 by Owain Glyndŵr.*

rebellion, increasing the fluidity of the land market and offering greater opportunities for the acquisition of land and income. Consolidated farms were appearing and small estates replacing the scattered hamlets of the tribal townships. English methods of conveyancing were adopted. The recovery of town life was also occurring at centres such as Ruthin and Oswestry: property was being rebuilt and repaired, the population was increasing, especially among Welsh inhabitants, and trade was being channelled increasingly through the towns. A variety of go-ahead men – gentry, burgesses, clerics and prosperous peasants – all took full advantage of the new sources of wealth. Families such as the Herberts, the Vaughans, the Gruffydds of Penrhyn, the Maurices of Clenennau, and the Mostyns all did extraordinarily well, acquiring land, office and prosperity, and creating the nuclei of a number of substantial landed estates. Others to enjoy prosperity were the affluent burgesses of the towns, numerous wealthy clergymen and some of the more substantial yeomen. For even the poorer classes difficulties were less acute than they were to become in the sixteenth century.

## Government, law and order

The fifteenth century witnessed widespread lawlessness and disorder as is reflected in both literary works and official documents. Some of Glyndŵr's followers survived by becoming outlaws, while soldiers, skilled in bloodshed and pillage, returning from the wars in France and survivors from the battles of the Wars of the Roses, such as the famous Dafydd ap Siancyn, added to their number. The breakdown of authority was especially marked in the Marches where records abound of personal attacks, rapes and murders, arson and organized raids on towns, highway robbery, cattle-stealing, kidnapping, assaults upon merchants and piracy in the Severn estuary. Problems were compounded by the lack of direct involvement and interest of many of the lords Marcher in their Welsh estates, the overwhelming difficulties facing the fifteenth-century English monarchy, failure to hold the Courts of Great Sessions regularly, and official reluctance to involve the rising Welsh squirearchy in the administration of both Crown and Marcher lands. Even in the Crown lands public order had collapsed by mid-century. Efforts were made to remedy matters. In 1437–8 and 1442–3 the Crown attempted to reach agreement with the lords Marcher to restore order, and in 1453 investigated the conduct of the officials of the Principality of North Wales. During the 1470s Edward IV created a business council to supervise the affairs of Wales.

Henry Tudor's victory over Richard III at Bosworth in 1485 led to great expectations from the Welsh. It was widely felt in Wales that at last a true Welshman by origins and upbringing ruled in London, a Welshman who was the son of prophecy, the heir to Owain Glyndŵr, and who was destined to fulfil the dream of Welsh supremacy over the island of Britain. Certainly, an unprecedented number of Welshmen received patronage and high office (among them, the David Cecil whose grandson William Cecil, Lord Burghley, became Elizabeth I's great minister). Henry did little, however, to redeem his promises to the Welsh more generally. Such reforms as took place were legal and administrative, especially the gradual removal of the statutory disabilities imposed in 1401–2 by Henry

IV. Wales remained in turmoil. The administration of both criminal and civil law relied overmuch upon local customary practice. More and more Marcher lordships had become Crown property, while three Counties Palatine – Pembroke, Glamorgan and Flint – were governed directly by the sovereign. Yet some lordships still remained in private hands. In 1493 Arthur, Prince of Wales, was given wide judicial powers in Wales and the Marches. The Council of Wales and the Marches based at Ludlow was formally brought into existence in 1501, entrusted to enforce law and order in the border areas and to prevent wrong-doers and outlaws from fleeing from one lordship to another to escape punishment. Such policies were inevitably piecemeal, highly inconsistent and largely ineffective. It was apparent that a radical, standardizing approach was required – the abolition of the March and the establishment of a uniform administrative structure. This was eventually achieved by the Union legislation of 1536 and 1543.

# 4

# Post-Union Wales

## *The Acts of Union*

By the sixteenth century the legal assimilation of Wales and England was completed. The Acts of Union of 1536 and 1543 can be portrayed as the culmination of a drive to extend the authority of the English Crown over Wales. Union had really been achieved by the Statute of Wales in 1284. During the intervening centuries the king had become by far the most powerful landowner, holding in his own possession a large majority of the lordships. Moreover Wales had become closely integrated with England in social and economic terms; the increasing disintegration of the manorial system and of Welsh tenurial institutions such as the *gwely* had led to an increasing emphasis on individualism in economic activity and social life. The emergence of large farms and consolidated estates, the expansion of trade and industry, and the evolution of commercial values closely paralleled contemporary developments in England. Wales was certainly well prepared for the kind of changes embodied in the Union legislation.

The Act of 1536, drawn up by the administration of Henry VIII's Secretary, Thomas Cromwell, abolished the Marcher lordships: some were assigned to existing Welsh and some to English counties such as Shropshire, Hereford and Gloucester, and the remainder blocked together to form the five new counties of Brecknock (Brecon), Denbigh, Monmouth, Montgomery and Radnor. To some extent the Act remained faithful to the boundaries of the former Marcher lordships. Linguistic divisions were not considered. Minor

*Conclusion*

adjustments to boundaries were made by the Act of 1543. A commission was to be set up to consider the subdivision of the shires into hundreds. Welshmen were to enjoy legal equality with Englishmen; the penal legislation of 1401–2 was superseded. 'Sinister usages and customs' were to be eliminated, and Welshmen allowed to 'have, enjoy and inherit' as Englishmen. Most importantly, land was to be inherited 'after the English tenure without division or partition', thus removing a major grievance of the Welsh throughout the later Middle Ages.

But Wales was not fully absorbed into England in legal affairs. It retained its own system of law courts which was extended into the new counties. The country was divided into four circuits for the Courts of Great Sessions, with each circuit comprising three counties. Regional chanceries and exchequers were established at Brecon and Denbigh and those already in existence at Caernarfon and Carmarthen confirmed. This system survived until its abolition in 1830. Monmouthshire, because of its location, was attached to the Oxford judicial circuit. Hence evolved the anomalous position which the county was to hold for many centuries, neither quite Welsh nor quite English. All administrative and judicial proceedings throughout Wales were to be conducted in English, and the records of the courts kept in Latin. All officials were to be English-speaking.

Each of the Welsh shires was granted parliamentary representation: two members for Monmouthshire, one each for every other county, and one member for all the ancient boroughs within a county except Merioneth. In 1543 the town of Haverfordwest was recognized as a county in its own right. The knights of the shire were to be paid wages, and burgesses of the ancient boroughs were to be responsible for the wages of the borough members, thus introducing the system of contributory boroughs unique to Wales. The forty-shilling freeholders enjoyed the franchise in the shires, while in the boroughs freemen alone could vote.

The Council of Wales and the Marches at Ludlow, formally re-established by Henry VII, was confirmed by the Act of 1543. It was made up of the Lord President, his deputy and twenty-two members, all royal nominees. It acted as a court of appeal and as a

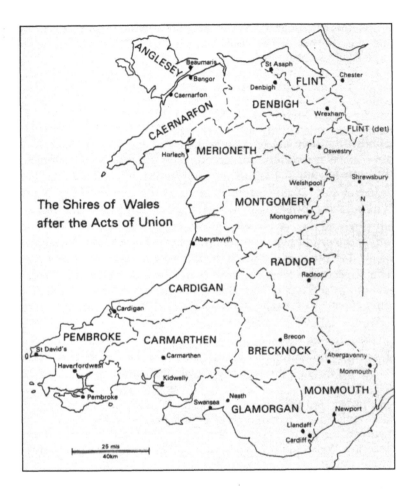

The Shires of Wales
after the Acts of Union

supervisory administrative body, responsible for the implementation
of Acts of Parliament and the appointment of senior shire officers
such as sheriffs and justices of the peace. Its authority extended over
the thirteen Welsh counties and five border counties, but the latter
group was allowed to break away from its jurisdiction in 1604. The
Council was suspended in 1641, revived in 1660 and finally dissolved
by statute in 1689.

*conclusion*

All too often the Union legislation is now portrayed as the beginning of the end of Wales and the Welsh. The Welsh language was proscribed for almost all official and legal purposes; English law replaced the native laws of Hywel Dda; a widening cleavage between the gentry, rapidly becoming Anglicized, and the lower orders of Welsh society soon sprang up; the evolution of a London-based culture soon eclipsed Welsh cultural life; and Wales was almost abolished as a separate administrative entity. But at the time the acts were widely welcomed, especially by the gentry, the commercial classes, lawyers and religious reformers. The Welsh had achieved full equality before the law with their English neighbours, a more stable, peaceful life with a major diminution in lawlessness ensued, and there emerged improved opportunities for individual advancement in the new economic climate. Numerous Welshmen flocked to London and made their fortunes as lawyers, merchants, shopkeepers, brewers and craftsmen. The Acts of Union, whether viewed as acts of emancipation or of oppression, certainly marked a fateful break with the past. They must be judged as part and parcel of Tudor policy for Wales as a whole. Thomas Cromwell's intention in formulating the Acts was not specifically to destroy the Welsh language and nationality but rather to create a united, centralized kingdom through the agency of the English language.

## Tudor shire administration

The shire, or county, was the basic unit of post-Union administration; its chief officer was the sheriff, chosen annually by the Council of Wales and the Marches. The sheriff initially performed a wide range of duties – legal administration outside the courts, the assessment and collection of taxes, the defence of the shire against the king's enemies and the conduct of parliamentary elections. There were two coroners in each shire, charged with the safeguarding of Crown finances and the administration of criminal law. The establishment of Justices of the Peace was a further Tudor innovation. Eight justices were to be chosen for every shire, each having an annual income from property of at least £20 a year and being fully conversant with the laws of the land. Acting as individual justices or in quarter sessions, held every three months, and special sessions, they tried and sentenced a wide range of offenders and performed many administrative duties: the maintenance of bridges and gaols, the setting of wages, the inspection of weights, measures and the quality of goods, the licensing of alehouses, and the supervision of poor relief. Each shire was further divided into hundreds, each in the care of a resident JP who was responsible for the appointment of two constables. A number of minor courts also continued to operate: the freeholders' or county court was held monthly by the sheriff and the hundred courts were conducted every two or three weeks, while borough courts and court leets survived in large numbers to deal with minor offences. The churchwardens, who were chosen by the parishioners, not only supervised church affairs, but together with the constables elected annually two surveyors of highways and recruited unpaid labour for repairs to roads. From 1601 the church-wardens and other householders were required by statute to give assistance to the sick, poor and aged, to compel the able-bodied poor to work and to apprentice pauper children. The church-wardens and other overseers were also responsible for the collection and distribution of a compulsory poor rate. This structure survived largely intact until the nineteenth century when it was forced to change by the demands of industrialization, urbanization and the march of democracy.

## The Reformation

The planting, nurturing and sustaining of Protestantism in Wales was a long process extending over three centuries. At the beginning of the sixteenth century the Christian faith may have been practised by almost all the Welsh, yet it was but vaguely understood, fostered by habit rather than conviction. The Reformation in Wales was certainly not of the people's making; it was imposed on them by King Henry VIII's government. Between 1529 and 1534 a series of major anti-papal statutes enacted by the Reformation Parliament deprived Pope Clement VII of the power he had previously enjoyed which was transferred to the King, who became Supreme Head of the Church in England and Wales. The Act of Supremacy of 1534 required the clergy and laymen in authority to swear an oath of loyalty to the Supreme Head. Two alone of all the clergy in Wales refused. The loyalty of the Welsh was important to the Crown because of the danger of invasion through Wales by the Roman Catholic powers, particularly in view of the proximity of Wales to an unstable and still largely 'Catholic' Ireland.

Secondly, the King and his advisers, anxious to exploit the financial possibilities of their new authority, took steps to dissolve the monasteries and to transfer their assets to the hands of the Crown. There were some fifty abbeys and friaries in Wales, many of them of the Cistercian order. Commissioners were sent out in 1535 to inquire into the state of the monasteries and to prepare a record of monastic income called the *Valor Ecclesiasticus*. As all the religious houses in Wales were found to have an income of less than £200 a year, they were suppressed in 1536, although Neath, Whitland and Strata Florida were permitted to continue until 1539. The same fate befell the friaries and other religious establishments in 1538. The rising gentry acquired much of their lands on favourable leases. Some monks and abbots received pensions; others became parish priests. Many buildings were allowed to become ruins. Most Welshmen displayed an attitude of unenthusiastic acceptance towards these changes, partly because by this time the monasteries, lacking in morale and enthusiasm and with depleted numbers, were but a shadow of their former selves, incapable of giving a lead or of inspiring devotion.

## Cistercian houses

The magnificent abbey built by the Cistercians at Tintern in the centre of the Wye valley is now one of the most famous monastic ruins in Britain. The monks may even have mined for iron and coal here, as is also true of Margam Abbey, founded by Robert Consul, Earl of Gloucester, in 1147. The most impressive part of the romantic abbey ruins at Margam is the twelve sided Chapter House which has a particularly fine doorway. On a hill behind are the ruins of Hen Eglwys, built as a place of worship and prayer for the local people who were not allowed to make use of the abbey. The ruins of Neath abbey are much less impressive. Four miles along the Dee estuary from Flint Castle are the picturesque ruins of Basingwerk Abbey, originally founded for monks of the order of Savigny who subsequently amalgamated with the Cistercians. Whitland became the mother house of the order in Wales. The ruins of Strata Florida Abbey stand near the village of Pontrhydfendigaid in Dyfed. Several Welsh princes and poets lie buried there. Strata Marcella lies three miles north-east of Welshpool. Abbey Cwmhir near the Clywedog brook in Powys has no more than low stone walls and a few bases of piers to be seen today. Here the headless body of Llywelyn the Last was received for burial. It was one of the largest abbeys in fourteenth-century Wales before being attacked by Owain Glyndŵr in 1401 and despoiled again at the Reformation.

The brief reign of Edward VI (1547–53), who had been brought up under the influence of two fervent Protestants, the Dukes of Somerset and Northumberland, saw the Protestant revolution proceed apace. There were sweeping raids on Church property – church plate, ornaments and chantries were ruthlessly swept away; images and pictures were shattered; many traditional saints' days and ceremonies were abrogated; simple tables replaced majestic altars. Above all, the English and Protestant Book of Common Prayer took the place of the Latin and Catholic rite, a particular problem in Wales where English was not the everyday language.

Although some contemporary poetry reflects a sense of outrage towards these changes, no rebellion took place in Wales against the Reformation. This fact may be attributed to Welsh loyalty to the Tudors, a lack of leadership from the clergy, the unwillingness of the gentry to rebel against a situation from which they might profit, and the very geographical remoteness and intellectual backwardness of Wales. Above all else, the acceptance reflected the truth that the ethics of neither Catholicism nor Protestantism had penetrated deeply into the consciousness of the Welsh. To most of them religion was a ritualized way of life rather than a code of profound philosophical beliefs.

The reign of Queen Mary (1553–8) saw a royally directed return to Rome, a dramatic change generally welcomed by the Welsh. In spite of Mary's vigorous persecution, there were only three Protestant martyrs throughout Wales, all English-speaking: Robert Ferrar, Rawlins White and William Nichol. Bishop Anthony Kitchin, often accused of despoiling the see of Llandaff, was able yet again to stretch his conscience sufficiently to accept the new order. He served as Bishop of Llandaff from 1545 until 1563. The gentry were permitted to retain the gains they had made from former Church property. A tiny number of hard-core Protestants, such as Richard Davies, convinced of the truth of their doctrine, went into exile in Europe, while others, such as William Salesbury, remained discreetly in hiding. But large numbers of priests were deprived of their livings in the dioceses of St Davids and Bangor following the passage of a decree prohibiting married men from saying mass after 20 December 1553.

Under Elizabeth, the daughter of Protestant humanism and the idol of the anti-Marian Londoners, a compromise settlement was enforced in the Act of Supremacy and the Act of Uniformity, both passed in 1559. The former measure established royal control over the Church subject to the authority of Parliament; the latter enforced the use of the Protestant Prayer Book, but one which differed substantially from that of 1552. Elizabeth trod a cautious middle path between identifying her Church too closely with the State and creating a radical Protestant Church as demanded by the returned exiles, and thus won the support of the moderate majority in Wales as elsewhere. In 1563 an Act of Parliament was passed compelling the Welsh bishops to provide a translation into Welsh of the Bible and the Book of Common Prayer, and to ensure that a copy of each should be placed in every church by 1 March 1567. The translations of the New Testament and Book of Common Prayer which appeared in 1567 were largely the work of William Salesbury, an Oxford-educated literary lawyer, assisted by Dr Richard Davies and Thomas Huet. A Welsh translation of the whole Bible, the work of Bishop

William Morgan, a Cambridge graduate and vicar of Llanrhaeadr ym Mochnant, was published in 1588, an event of crucial importance for the survival of the Welsh language as it made Welsh the language of public worship. Assisted by the Welsh poet Edmwnd Prys, Morgan produced a literary classic, renowned for the beauty and purity of its language, and a model for all subsequent prose writers in Welsh.

### William Salesbury

Born c. 1520 at Llansannan, Denbighshire, a member of the Salesbury family of Lleweni. He was educated at Oxford University, where he steeped himself in Reformation and Renaissance ideas, and possibly at the Inns of Court. He produced a large number of literary works from 1547 to 1552 including *Kynniver Llith a Bann* (1551), a Welsh translation of the Epistles and Gospels of the Book of Common Prayer. He spent much time in London, became fully aware of the importance of the printing press and developed a deep love of the Welsh language and a consciousness of the threats posed to it. Forced to go into hiding during the reign of Queen Mary, he became friendly with Bishop Richard Davies after the accession of Elizabeth. He joined Bishop Davies at Abergwili to work on the translation of the Book of Common Prayer and the New Testament, both of which were published in 1567. Salesbury's linguistic oddities to some extent undermined the success of these achievements. He fully intended to produce a translation of the Old Testament, but published nothing after 1567. He died in 1584.

One ardent reformer of the Elizabethan age was John Penry, a native of Llangamarch in Breconshire, educated at Cambridge and Oxford, who implored Queen and Parliament that the Welsh should be taught in their mother tongue. Highly critical of the organization of the Church, he was wrongly suspected of being the author of the infamous *Martin Marprelate Tracts*, which virulently attacked episcopacy, and was executed for treason in 1593, the first Welsh Puritan martyr.

## William Morgan

Born in 1545, the son of a tenant on the Gwydir estate. He was educated at Cambridge University, where he became fully involved in the Puritan controversies of the age and met Edmwnd Prys, Richard Vaughan and Gabriel Goodman. He became vicar of Llanbadarn Fawr in 1572 and incumbent of Llanrhaeadr-ym-Mochnant in 1578, where he began to translate the Bible into Welsh, having won the staunch support of Archbishop Whitgift. He completed the work in 1588, having spent a year in London. His translation was skilful, accurate, artistic and sensitive. Its appearance ensured that the purity and strength of the poetic vocabulary should survive, and above all it prevented the Welsh language from degenerating into a number of dialects and perhaps from dying out completely. In 1595 he became Bishop of Llandaff, where he revised his translation and published a new edition of the Prayer Book. He was moved to St Asaph in 1601 and completed a new version of the New Testament. He may also have compiled a Welsh dictionary. He died in 1604. A memorial to the translators of the Welsh Bible stands outside the cathedral, but Morgan's burial place is unmarked.

Catholics such as Morris Clynnog and Gruffydd Robert, who had fled to the Continent on Elizabeth's accession, hoped to restore Wales to the old faith through foreign invasion and replacing the Queen with Mary Queen of Scots. But such men, called recusants, were always few in number in Wales, confined primarily to the English border and the north-east. Two of their number, Richard White in 1584 and William Davies in 1593, suffered martyrdom for their faith. By the end of Elizabeth's reign in 1603, although Wales was first and foremost a Protestant country, Catholic practices did persist especially in remote areas, as is reflected in the keeping of vigils, the cherishing of images and relics, and the visiting of holy wells and other shrines. There was simply an inadequate number of sufficiently reliable and educated priests in Wales to teach the basic tenets of Anglicanism in the parishes. For many Welshmen religious observance remained an amalgam of custom, superstition, dread of the supernatural and of man's fate after death, and a basic knowledge of some Bible stories. And so matters continued until the eighteenth century.

## *Agriculture*

The Welsh economy remained basically pastoral – the rearing of animals – stunted by a lack of capital and enterprise, by primitive technology, by ineffective means of marketing, and by an excess of unskilled labourers. Prospects of achieving economic prosperity were further undermined by the nature of the terrain and soil, the unfavourable damp climate, bad or indifferent harvests, disease and illness, localism, and a marked reluctance to embark upon technical and scientific improvements. Livestock farming was of vital importance; the sale of cattle and wool gave the majority of Welsh farmers most of their cash incomes. Cattle-trading between Wales and England, originating in the medieval period, increased spectacularly in the sixteenth and seventeenth centuries – 'the Spanish Fleet of Wales which brings hither the little gold and silver we have'. Cattle were driven to fairs and bought by dealers who drove them to English markets. These drovers became men of considerable status and substance within their communities. The sixteenth century also witnessed a great rise in the price of wool which became more important in the economy, as sheep were well suited to the pasture of the Welsh hillsides. Welsh woollen cloth was regarded as coarse and inferior, a reflection of a cottage-based industry. But English cloth merchants attended Welsh fairs for the purchase of wool and cloth which they conveyed to English centres for further working. The cloth trade came to be based at Oswestry, dominated by the powerful Shrewsbury Drapers' Company.

Trade in corn also flourished in the late sixteenth century, especially from south Wales to England and Ireland. Oats alone were grown on the bleak hillsides, but wheat and barley crops flourished in the fertile valleys especially in the southern coastal areas, the use of lime facilitating intensive working and reasonable productivity. Butter and cheese were marketed in small quantities from Wales. This period saw the creation of compact, consolidated farms and the enclosure of common arable land, meadow and pasture alike, even of the rough pasture of the highlands. Enclosure of this rough pasture was deeply resented and led to disturbances in some areas where the peasantry tore down the enclosing fences erected by the gentry, disturbances which were recorded in the proceedings of local courts.

## Industry

A similar lack of initiative and investment stifled industrial development and trade, although investment by English prospectors and metal manufacturers increased after Union. The mining of coal increased sharply in Flintshire, Pembrokeshire and western Glamorgan, especially for the smelting of non-ferrous metals. Coal seams near the surface were worked intensively. Neath and Swansea exported substantial quantities of coal to Bristol, Ireland, the Channel Islands and western France. Coal accounted for ninety per cent of Welsh exports by the end of the seventeenth century.

The iron industry, too, was in swift expansion, exploiting the natural resources of Wales – its timber and water power – and encouraged by the long struggle with Spain and by the readiness of English ironmasters, such as Sir William Sydney and Thomas Mynyffee, to augment local enterprise with capital and technical skill. An initial wide dispersal of mines and furnaces through Wales gave way to a concentration near the coalfields where the major iron ore reserves were located, especially in the Glamorgan and Monmouthshire valleys, the latter established by Richard Hanbury, and in the Chirk area. Before the eighteenth century, however, copper was the most important metal to be produced in Wales, pursued in scattered locations in the west and north-west of the country. Thomas Thurland and the German Daniel Hochstetter were, in 1564, given the right to search for copper and other precious metals in Wales. In north Cardiganshire copper and lead-mining were combined. In the 1580s Thomas Smith was granted a lease of the lead-mines in Cardiganshire of the Society of Mines Royal, a joint stock company formed in 1568. These mines were subsequently leased by Hugh Myddelton in 1617, and soon provided him with a net income of £2,000 a month. Lead-mining

*The title-page of Bishop William Morgan's translation of the Bible of 1588, the first complete Bible in the Welsh language.*

also took place in Flintshire in a narrow belt from Diserth to Wrexham. Some mines produced silver, particularly the Cardiganshire valleys to the west of the Plynlymon range. Slate was quarried in north-west Wales, and enjoyed important domestic markets in England and Ireland. By 1688 over one million slates had been exported. Although Wales in 1700 was by no means an industrialized nation, it possessed a range of small manufacturing and extractive industries and the embryos of larger concentrations which awaited the extensive capital investment and the novel technologies of the industrial age.

## Welsh society

At the accession of Henry VIII in 1509 the population of Wales was about 250,000. Most of these were Welsh-speaking, illiterate, rural dwellers, with a modest standard of living. The lives of most of them were governed by purely local factors, and this is seen in farming practices, prices, weights and measures, folk traditions, domestic architecture and often distinct dialects. Communities were isolated, unaware of national events, while most individuals ventured outside their native villages only once or twice in a lifetime. Soldiers, sailors, merchants and their servants were the only members of the lower orders of society to have travelled extensively. Communal co-operation and interdependence were to some extent undermined by local disputes, feuds and general mistrust, themselves largely the product of dire poverty, illness, disease and sudden tragedy. Life for many was harsh and short. Society was strictly hierarchical and deferential; the landed classes were firmly at the apex in Church and State. There was a fundamental distinction between the 'gentle' or upper classes – no more than some three per cent of the population – and the great mass of peasantry and landless people.

## *The gentry*

The class of squires which emerged in post-Union society was to dominate Welsh life until the end of the nineteenth century. To this gentry class, ancestry was important; a few were descended from the Welsh princes and *uchelwyr*. For those who were not so well-descended, there are many examples of the concoction on behalf of a 'new' gentry family of an impressive pedigree by a devious herald or genealogist. The possession of wealth was of even greater importance, usually displayed publicly in a grand mansion, extensive grounds, a large number of servants and a luxurious lifestyle. The decay of tribalism in the 'Welsh areas' and of the manorial system in the south and border laid the foundations of many gentry estates. These foundations were strengthened by trading activities in the towns, the decline of the greater nobility, the widespread availability of former monastic land at the dissolution of the monasteries, the ruthless deprivation of the peasantry of much of its land, the enclosure of large tracts of moorland and common, and encroachment on Crown lands.

In these ways did such families as the Maurices of Clenennau, the Barlows of Slebech in Pembrokeshire, the Pryses of Gogerddan, the Herberts of Swansea, the Mostyns of Flint, the Bulkeleys of Beaumaris and, above all, the Wynns of Gwydir build up their estates. Such families came to enjoy considerable authority and prestige. They controlled the administration of local justice which gave them power within the county and enabled them to line their own pockets through exploiting their authority. They prudently made marriage alliances to add to their estates and to consolidate their power and position in local society. These families were linked by an intricate web of matrimonial alliances. They formed a self-conscious status group, ever anxious to increase their incomes through improving the running of their home farms and especially by extending the area they controlled, efforts rendered vital by rampant inflation. They took a great interest in antiquarianism and the workings of English law and litigation. They welcomed Anglicizing influences – the English language, English attitudes and

English family connections gained an important foothold in Wales. They visited their county towns, and occasionally centres such as Ludlow, Chester, Bristol and London.

Many of the sons of the gentry received their education in English schools, but grammar schools were founded in Wales at this time – a royal licence for the establishment of Christ College, Brecon, was granted in 1541. Other grammar schools opened their doors at Ruthin, Bangor, Cowbridge, Margam, Llanrwst, Presteigne, Beaumaris, Wrexham and Carmarthen. All were a strong Anglicizing influence; the education they offered was strictly classical. In 1571 Jesus College, Oxford, was founded by Dr Hugh Price of Brecon to cater for the needs of Welshmen. Some Welsh students went to Cambridge, and many trained for a legal career at the Inns of Court, Lincoln's Inn and Gray's Inn.

## The lower orders of society

Sixteenth-century farmers were termed either yeomen (substantial farmers) or husbandmen (small farmers). Social acceptance by one's peers was essential before one was considered a yeoman. It was yeomen who generally served as churchwardens, as overseers of the poor or of highways and as high constables of hundreds. Many elected the knights of the shire. Husbandmen, although sometimes becoming petty or parish constables, normally made up the 'sort of men who do not rule'. Many of them lived close to subsistence level and had no reserve capital.

Society also included increasing numbers of labourers, vagrants and paupers. The JPs fixed annually at Easter the wages of many of the working classes by the provisions of the Statute of Artificers of 1563, and they were reluctant to raise them. Farm labourers enjoyed no security in their posts, often being employed for only a year at a time. Unattached labourers, the poor and impotent, vagabonds, cottagers and children old enough to be apprenticed were rigidly supervised and controlled by parish officers. Many paupers and vagrants were hounded ruthlessly and punished, often being condemned to the infamous houses of correction. Mobility of labour was restricted as much as possible. For much of Welsh society, existence was at best humdrum, hard and precarious. Many Welsh people were the victims of the state of the harvest, population growth and rampant inflation, and of primitive and underdeveloped farming techniques.

# 5

# Stuart Wales

## *The Stuarts*

The accession of James I in 1603 was warmly received in Wales. He was welcomed as a descendant of Henry Tudor, as a worthy successor to Queen Elizabeth, whose blessing he had received, and as the upholder of the Tudor monarchy and regime. He was certainly considered by far preferable to a representative of Spain, who would undoubtedly have jeopardized the prospects of the many Welshmen serving the State, the law, the Church and the aristocratic households. Moreover, the disastrous failure in 1601 of the rash uprising of the Earl of Essex (who had built up a formidable following among the Welsh gentry) encouraged many Welshmen to turn to the Crown for favour and patronage. Although some Catholics plotted to seize James and to attempt to free him from Protestant influences, their schemes came to nothing. The failure of the Gunpowder Plot heralded the inglorious end of political Catholicism. James, fully appreciative of Welsh sympathy and support, conferred offices, honours and favours upon large numbers of Welshmen, among them Rowland Meyrick, Sir John Vaughan of Golden Grove, Sir Robert Vaughan of Llwydiarth, Sir Robert Mansel and Sir John Herbert. The new king claimed the success of the Union legislation as a compelling argument for a similar measure for Scotland, and praised lavishly the 'loyalty, faith and obedience' of the Welsh constituents represented by Members of Parliament who 'served for the country of Wales'. The Council of Wales was widely viewed as a symbol of Welsh autonomy and focus of national unity. In many ways, James's reign appeared a continuation of Elizabeth's; the idea of a common British citizenship was enthusiastically accepted by most of the Welsh gentry.

## Early Stuart politics

The conclusion of hostilities with Spain, and the ending of the crippling demands of war on men and money, brought a profound sense of relief to the Welsh. The administrative structure of the sixteenth century remained intact, monopolized as previously by a small group of leading county families. The Council of Wales maintained its surveillance of law, order and jurisdiction, powerfully supported by James who viewed its continued existence as a useful defence of his own royal prerogative and an effective means of curbing the excesses of the most powerful among the Welsh gentry, particularly Sir John Wynn.

The attendance of Welsh representatives at Westminster constituted a vital link between Wales and London, ensuring the widespread circulation of news and information. Some Members of Parliament took pains to sound the opinions of leading constituents before proceeding to London. Politics invariably continued to revolve around county personalities and issues; few Welsh MPs intervened in Commons debates and contested elections were rare. Even when a contest took place the election campaign centred on local struggles for power, honour and pre-eminence, where serious issues of high political principle found no place. There was, however, a tendency for the Welsh MPs to vote and act as a group in the Commons on questions of relevance to Wales, especially over financial matters such as the imposition of unpopular taxes. The application of the royal right of purveyance – the compulsory purchase by the king's purveyors of Welsh cattle at nominal prices – was deeply resented and gave rise to a storm of protest from the chief cattle-raising counties.

*Gwydir in Gwynedd, the home of Sir John Wynn and later part
of the estates of the Williams-Wynn dynasty.*

## The Church

Continuity is also much in evidence in a consideration of the history
of the Church, which James regarded as a powerful buttress to the
authority of the Crown. Anglicanism was by this time warmly
embraced by the majority. Worship and instruction through the
medium of the Welsh language had become more and more familiar.
Many important works had been translated into Welsh. These
included the 'Book of Homilies', published in Welsh in 1606 by
Edward James, a Glamorgan cleric. The year 1620 saw an outstanding
translation of the Authorized Version of the Bible and a new Prayer
Book, the work of Bishop Richard Parry and Dr John Davies,
Mallwyd. A metrical translation of the Psalms by Edmwnd Prys
followed in 1621, while new editions of the revered *Llyfr Plygain*
were published regularly. The five-shilling Bible, *y Beibl Bach*,
appeared in 1630 in 500 copies. Between 1629 and 1634 Sir Thomas

Myddelton and Rowland Heylyn financed the publication of a large number of cheap devotional works in Welsh. These were within the reach of the reasonably well-to-do. There is evidence of the widespread use of Welsh in sermons at least in the two north Wales dioceses.

Above all, perhaps, there was the work of Rees Prichard of Llandovery, widely known as 'the old Vicar', who became Chancellor of St Davids in 1626. Between 1615 and 1635 he composed simple rhymes, easily committed to memory, which provided basic religious instruction. The rhymes comprised extracts from the Scriptures, fundamental Church doctrines and homely advice for everyone on tackling life's difficulties. The influence of Prichard's work was immense especially in south-west Wales; he made Protestantism available to those classes who could not appreciate the Psalms of Edmwnd Prys and who could neither afford to buy nor read the Bible. Most of his verses were memorized and passed from person to person. Even illiterate folk could recite large numbers of them. Although Prichard died in 1644, the first selection of his verses was not published until 1659. A complete collection followed in 1672, while the title *Canwyll y Cymry* ('The Welshmen's Candle') was used for the work from 1681. Fourteen editions had been published by 1730.

Yet the shortcomings of the established Church kept moral and religious standards generally low in Wales. Many Englishmen were appointed bishops of Llandaff and St Davids in south Wales; these in turn often chose English incumbents separated from their parishioners by the gulf of language. The Welsh Church remained poor; pluralism and non-residence were rife. There were far too few preachers, while pastoral duties such as visiting the sick, baptizing infants and even burying the dead were widely neglected. Many of the clergy were accused of turning a blind eye to bigamy and adultery. Superstitious practices were as much in evidence as ever, and games, dancing and ballad-singing, even the frequenting of alehouses, on a Sunday were practised regularly.

## Early Puritans

Wales, a poor, undeveloped nation, with a small middle class, inevitably proved generally unreceptive to Puritanism which was widely regarded as an alien importation. It prospered only in the border area and in the towns of the south, spreading from Bristol to Monmouthshire and, along commercial routes, to Carmarthen in the west and Chester in the north-east. Links between Bristol and Pembrokeshire also bore fruit. Many London-Welsh merchants played an important philanthropic role by financing the education and clothing of poor children, the setting up of schools and workhouses, and the circulation of bibles and devotional works. In 1626 a group of London tradesmen and lawyers formed the Feoffees for Impropriations which strove to purchase the patronage of vacant Church livings in order that they might be filled with Puritan ministers. Almost £7,000 were raised and thirty-one ecclesiastical livings purchased and filled by 1633, a number of them on the Welsh borders. This promising scheme was destroyed by Archbishop Laud in 1633. But the plight of Wales continued to feature prominently in the interests of many London Welshmen who sponsored the publication of devotional works in Welsh and of translations of the most important Puritan works by authors such as Lewis Bayly, Arthur Dent and William Perkins.

As the 1630s progressed it became apparent that the Puritan campaign was suffering because of the uncompromising enmity of Archbishop Laud. But a small group of Welsh Puritans was prepared to challenge Laud, foremost among them William Wroth, a native of Abergavenny who in 1617 became rector of Llanfaches in Monmouthshire – the Welsh county most accessible from London and Bristol – and William Erbery, incumbent of St Mary's, Cardiff, where the curate was Walter Cradock. Wroth and Erbery were brought before the Court of High Commission in 1635; Wroth fell into line by swearing obedience to his bishop in 1638 but Erbery resigned. Cradock was deprived of his licence and moved to Wrexham as a curate to spread the Gospel.

Other zealous Puritans joined forces with this small group on the Welsh borders; among them was Vavasor Powell, a restless and dynamic individual, a native of Knucklas in Radnorshire, who was converted by the preaching of Walter Cradock – as too was Morgan Llwyd, who became an outstanding writer and theologian. These men formed a close, warm-hearted brotherhood who preached extensively and to great effect on the Welsh borders. In November 1639 Henry Jesse was sent from London to assist Wroth and Cradock to set up an Independent Church at Llanfaches in Monmouthshire, a church established on the pattern of those founded by Puritan settlers in New England. Llanfaches became the mother church of Welsh Nonconformity and there, according to Erbery, 'all was spirit and life'. Alas, their sense of well-being was short-lived. At the outbreak of the Civil War in August 1642 the Puritan saints fled for their lives. This was indeed the time of the 'desolation of the Welsh Saints'.

### Morgan Llwyd

Born in 1619 at Cynfal Fawr, Maentwrog, Merioneth. He was educated at Wrexham where in 1635 he was converted by listening to Walter Cradock, then a local curate. With Cradock he moved to the first 'gathered church' at Llanfaches in 1639, joined the Parliamentary army in 1642 and saw service in southern England. In 1644 Parliament sent him as an itinerant preacher to north Wales. He settled at Wrexham, and in 1650 he became an Approver under the Act for the Propagation of the Gospel in Wales, charged to find suitable replacements for the ejected ministers. He was settled as minister of Wrexham parish church in 1656. He published eleven works, three in English and eight in Welsh, of which the most important is *Llyfr y Tri Aderyn* (1653). He was also an eloquent preacher in Welsh and English. His final years were clouded by personal tragedy and he died in 1659.

## Charles I

Relations between the King and his Welsh subjects became more strained than in the days of James I. Charles's demands for men and money to meet the challenge of the Catholic powers were initially readily met, but a reluctance to raise the men, money and ships demanded soon grew. Complaints arose that measures had been taken without parliamentary sanction. Charles's period of personal rule from 1629 to 1640 coincided with a succession of bad harvests, outbreaks of plague, high food prices, widespread depression and unemployment. The issue of the Book of Orders in January 1631 with its harsh enforcement of the poor law and control of food supplies and prices was widely resented in Wales. The annual enforcement from 1634 of the practice of raising Ship Money led to bitter resistance. In some Welsh counties not a penny was raised. There was further dissatisfaction as a result of the efforts of a number of bishops appointed to the Welsh dioceses by Laud to restore Arminian principles to their churches and services, one factor which led to an increase in the number of Welsh recusants and Puritans. There was ample latent opposition to Charles within Wales, opposition fuelled by his attempts to levy extensive Welsh troops to suppress a rebellion in Scotland against the enforcement of a new prayer book. The Welsh MPs were also much concerned with the question of monopolies, as the granting of a monopoly of the sale of Welsh cloth to the Shrewsbury Drapers' Company had been a major grievance in Wales. When the famous Long Parliament met for the first time in November 1640, a number of Welsh MPs were initially virulent in their attacks upon the King, the bishops and recusants such as the Earl of Worcester and the Montgomeryshire Herberts. Yet by 1642 it was apparent that most Welsh opinion had coalesced behind the King, and men and money were raised on his behalf in many Welsh counties.

## The First Civil War

In Wales the Puritans were insufficiently numerous to mount an effective opposition to the King. There was scarcely an urban middle class in Wales, while the leaders of Welsh society, the gentry, generally beneficiaries of the activities of the Council of Wales, supported the King's prerogative. The English part of

Pembrokeshire and some parts of Denbighshire alone supported Parliament against the King. Wales was indeed of especial importance to Charles. It was a secure refuge to which he might retreat when hard pressed in England. It was a useful recruiting ground – 'the nursery of the king's infantry' – and it formed a direct line of communication with Catholic Ireland; it was indeed a potential landing-ground for Irish troops. The Marquis of Worcester, whose seat was at Raglan Castle in Monmouthshire, placed his huge wealth at the King's disposal.

Men from Glamorgan played an active part in the Battle of Edgehill. In 1643 Welsh troops led by Sir John Owen of Clenennau aided at the capture of the Puritan city of Bristol. But the Royalists failed to take Gloucester and Hull as part of the same plan to launch a triple advance on London. At Nantwich in January 1644 the Parliamentary army routed the King's forces, a defeat which led to the placing of Prince Rupert in charge of all Welsh operations, to be assisted by Sir John Owen of Clenennau and Charles Gerard. Indeed, Gerard succeeded in recapturing Carmarthen and Haverfordwest. But the King's crushing defeat at Naseby in June led to his retreat to south Wales. At Cardiff he was besieged by the complaints of his own supporters about the plundering and looting of the countryside, the imposition of taxes, and the selection of Englishmen to command the King's troops. The Pembrokeshire Royalists were defeated at Colby Moor, and Carmarthen and Brecon were soon captured by Parliament. Only a few castles held out for the King; they fell one by one until Raglan was reduced in August 1646 and finally Harlech in March 1647.

## The Second Civil War

A quarrel between Parliament and the victorious army soon followed the end of the first Civil War and was of much consequence in Wales. The death of the Earl of Essex had meant that two of the Parliamentary leaders in south Pembrokeshire, Laugharne and Powell, were no longer automatically loyal to the army with whose religious views they disagreed. The third leader in the area, Poyer, disobeyed orders by refusing to disband those troops which had not been incorporated into the regular army, and he soon declared for the King, Parliament and the Scots, as indeed did Powell. Horton failed to suppress the revolt initially, but at the great Battle of St Fagans on 8 May 1648, Powell and Laugharne, although commanding 8,000 men, were routed by Horton at the head of 3,000 trained soldiers. A revolt which had broken out in north Wales led by Sir John Owen of Clenennau was crushed near Bangor on 5 June. Tenby soon surrendered to Horton and, after a siege which lasted seven weeks, Pembroke yielded to Cromwell himself who had assumed the leadership of the Welsh campaign. All three leaders were condemned to death when tried by court martial in London, but Poyer alone was executed.

### John Jones, Maesygarnedd

Born in c. 1597 as a member of the gentry family of Maesygarnedd in Ardudwy, Merioneth. He became a member of the Puritan household of Sir Hugh Myddelton in London. He fought for Parliament during the Civil War and progressed rapidly, taking part in the siege of Laugharne in 1644 and the siege of Chester in 1645. He became Colonel in 1646 and Member of Parliament for Merioneth in 1647. He was also a Commissioner for the Propagation of the Gospel in Wales from 1650 to 1653. His second wife was a sister to Oliver Cromwell, who was himself the great-great-grandson of Morgan Williams of Glamorgan, one of the many Welshmen lured to London by the prospect of a fortune, who became an ale brewer at Putney. Jones was a close associate of the leaders of the Puritan movement in Wales. He had been present at the trial of Charles I and was one of the signatories of his death warrant. He was executed on 17 October 1660.

## Wales and the Commonwealth

Two Welshmen were among those who signed the death warrant of Charles I – Thomas Wogan, MP for Cardigan Boroughs, and

Colonel John Jones of Maesygarnedd in Merioneth, who married Cromwell's sister. Few in Wales reaped comfort from the end of the hostilities for which they had yearned so passionately. Many Royalists inevitably found it difficult to accept the new regime, some being compelled to pay heavy fines and others suffering the sequestration of their estates. But these years did witness a participation in local government of classes in society previously excluded. Further, those who had supported the winning side in the war avidly took advantage of the opportunity to purchase lands readily available from sequestrations and sales, and became new county families of the first rank. The pattern of landownership in Wales was thus modified considerably. Above all, the years of the Interregnum saw a positive effort to puritanize the Welsh, an attempt which laid the basis for the later development of Nonconformity in Wales. This campaign also included a state-supported system of education never before attempted in Britain and not to be repeated until the nineteenth century.

## The Propagation of the Puritan Gospel

During the early years of the war Parliament recognized its obligation to provide godly ministers to evangelize 'the dark corners of the land' such as Wales. Between 1644 and 1649 130 clerics were appointed to livings in Wales to replace unworthy incumbents. Their efforts were supplemented by the preaching of peripatetic ministers; Parliament lent generous financial support to enable 'saints' such as Powell, Cradock, Llwyd, Symonds and Walter to evangelize along the Welsh borders. The Commonwealth attempted to puritanize Wales by the passage on 22 February 1650 of an Act for the Better Propagation and Preaching of the Gospel in Wales which appointed seventy-one Commissioners, most of them prominent officials who had displayed fidelity to the cause of Parliament, to investigate complaints against the clergy and to eject those whom they considered unfit. Within three years 278 clerics (196 in the south and 82 in the north) had been deprived of their livings for a range of offences ranging from pluralism to ignorance, drunkenness, keeping alehouses or simply supporting the King. A second group of twenty-five Approvers was set up by the Act to select 'godly and painful men' to fill the vacant livings. Their number included Cradock, Llwyd, Powell and John Miles, founder of the first Baptist church at Ilston in Glamorgan. But their task proved difficult, indeed impossible, and a system of itinerant preachers was forced upon them by the paucity of 'godly men' of whom they could approve.

In spite of this, the efforts of the Puritan 'saints' met with considerable success. Vavasor Powell, unrivalled in his preaching ability, energy and enthusiasm, regularly undertook preaching tours of a hundred miles a week. His colleagues enjoyed an influence and an appeal far in excess of their numbers. The Propagation Act also attempted to establish a national system of schools. The Approvers were charged with the task of appointing suitable schoolmasters. Sixty-three new schools were opened in the market towns of Wales (in addition to the Tudor grammar schools) where children of both sexes were taught to read, write and count without paying fees.

Yet complaints against the Commissioners became rife in Wales. A number of vocal pamphleteers such as Alexander Griffith virulently attacked this as an age of deprivation and spiritual desolation, the itinerant ministers as shameful tinkers and rogues, and the Commissioners as rulers by oppression. Indeed many Welshmen felt that they were living under an alien oppressive regime; the shadow of Cromwell's army lay across the campaigns of the Commissioners. As Colonel John Jones, Maesygarnedd, in attempting to justify the government's actions, put it, 'I had rather do a people good though against their wills, than please them in show only.' Many Puritan leaders in Wales, committed Fifth Monarchy men who believed that the reign of Christ on earth was now at hand, became vehement critics of the government, all the more so after Cromwell's adoption of the title of Lord Protector in 1653. Although Parliament did not renew the Commission in April 1653, in the following March the Committee of Triers was entrusted to choose suitable ministers throughout England and Wales. Some most gifted preachers influenced Welsh life during the

Commonwealth, and a number of Nonconformist sects, among them the Independents, the Baptists, the Fifth Monarchy Men and the Quakers, became firmly established in Wales for the first time in its history.

## The Restoration

When Charles II landed at Dover on 25 May 1660, the Welsh generally displayed jubilation and relief, reflecting a widespread yearning for peace, unity and stability. Many Royalist families regained the offices they had held previously and with them their former local prominence and prestige. A majority of Welsh Royalists and Churchmen returned to Parliament in 1661. Yet a legacy of bitterness and recrimination remained, as did an abiding fear of further upheaval and violence reflected in a determination to wreak vengeance on old enemies. Colonel John Jones was executed at Charing Cross on 17 October 1660. Cromwell was remembered as the wilful destroyer of sacred places and country houses, and Charles I extolled as a pure and upright saint, whose execution had been an outrageously evil deed, recalled on 30 January each year.

## Religious life: the Penal Code

The Restoration heralded the return of the Established Church as surely as the return of the king. There remained great hostility to Puritanism in Wales, one reason for the warm welcome given to Charles II. No more than about five per cent of the Welsh population were Puritans. Many Puritan ministers were deprived of their livings at once, others resigned voluntarily, and many suffered violent retribution. In all, 130 Puritan ministers left their livings, many being replaced by those who had themselves been ejected a decade earlier. An Act of Uniformity of April 1662 required all ministers to give their assent to the rites and liturgy of the Church, a measure which created an enduring and painful social division in Wales. A series of repressive measures called the 'Clarendon Code' was passed, which imposed severe penalties on those who refused to conform to the Established Church. In particular, the first Conventicle Act of May 1664 prohibited dissidents from assembling for religious worship in groups of more than five persons other than according to the practices of the Church. Severe penalties were enacted, including transportation for seven years for the third offence. The Five Mile Act of 1665 aimed at the destruction of Nonconformity in the towns, while the Test Act of 1673 disqualified Dissenters from holding office under the Crown unless they complied with a sacramental test. Although the penal legislation was often harshly enforced, many Nonconformists, especially Baptists and Independents, continued to meet in secret in isolated places and thus formed the core of many later Dissenting causes. The most unrelenting persecution was reserved for Roman Catholics and Quakers.

## The Toleration Act of 1689

Declarations of Indulgence were issued by James II in 1687 and 1688, and in May 1689 the Toleration Act allowed Dissenters to worship in licensed, unlocked meeting houses. Nonconformists could now worship in peace and build their own chapels. Yet they remained excluded from municipal government and the universities until the repeal of the Test and Corporation Acts in 1828. But it was during the late seventeenth century that Nonconformists planted the seeds of their phenomenal later growth; they were especially successful in large parishes and isolated communities where Church organization was at its weakest. Dissent was strongest in south Wales (some twelve per cent of the population by 1700), in commercial communities and Anglicized towns where large numbers of tradesmen, artisans and craftsmen joined its ranks, people of independent means and spirit, free from fear of retribution by the local squire and parson, people to whom the sober and dignified worship of the chapel appealed. They placed great stress on education and the achievement of literacy and many became nimble-minded and sharp-tongued philosophers and debaters. Their numbers remained small – some five per cent of the population of Wales by 1715–18 – but they enjoyed a disproportionate influence in their preaching, their chapel-building, in the production of religious literature and the instilling of Puritan values.

## The social scene

Wales remained an overwhelmingly rural country with a small population of some 370,000 in 1670, about one-sixth of which lived in towns. The population was growing, but not consistently, for runs of bad harvests and the vagaries of infectious diseases took their periodic toll. Impoverished upland areas were especially vulnerable to these natural crises. Rank, title and birth remained important, these in turn reflecting wealth and landholding. The fundamental division between the gentry and the common people remained, an index of the inequality and maldistribution of wealth.

The rise of the Welsh gentry continued apace. The prudent use of legal devices and cautious marriage settlements enabled the larger landowners to extend their lands, often at the expense of their less affluent and less powerful neighbours, many of whom became burdened by financial troubles. In the generation after the Restoration, the Welsh Titans emerged; the mightiest was Sir Watkin Williams Wynn of Wynnstay, followed by the Morgan family of Tredegar in Monmouthshire. Some families, such as the Pryses of Gogerddan in Cardiganshire, prospered by developing the mineral resources of their estates. The greater landowners came to dominate political life through sitting at Westminster. Some individuals, such as Sir John Vaughan of Trawscoed and Sir John Trevor of Trevalun, became figures of national importance, and, as a result, became increasingly Anglicized. But the Welsh MPs did not now act as a body in the Commons; they became part of the Court or of English political factions.

Some participated in the expansion of the English Empire: in 1612 Sir Thomas Button of Duffryn in Glamorgan landed in northern Canada while commanding an expedition to discover a north-west passage to Asia, while in 1620 Sir Robert Mansel of Margam, Vice-Admiral of England, was commissioned to suppress the corsairs of Algiers. Trading links and voyages of exploration led to plantations in foreign countries.

In spite of their increasing Anglicization, some of the Welsh gentry did contribute to the development of Welsh scholarship, foremost among them Robert Vaughan of Hengwrt in Merioneth, who assembled an outstanding library of Welsh books and manuscripts, and Dr John Davies of Mallwyd, who produced a Welsh grammar and dictionary.

## Great houses

Many of the mansions built by the Welsh nobility remain today. St Fagan's Castle, about 3.5 miles west of Cardiff and now the home of the National History Museum, is a multigabled Tudor building, really a fortified mansion which retains in its walls some of the stones of an early fortress built by Sir Peter le Sore. Just beyond the western outskirts of Newport is Tredegar House, described as 'the most splendid brick house of seventeenth-century Wales'. Near Crickhowell in Powys is Tretower Court, a well-restored, fourteenth-century, fortified manor house, adjoining which are the ruins of the twelfth-century castle built by the Normans to guard the Usk valley from the Welsh. Gogerddan, a mansion in the parish of Trefeurig near Aberystwyth and the home of the Pryse family, is now the site of the Welsh Plant Breeding Station. Some 1.5 miles from the centre of Welshpool is Trelydan Hall, a picturesque, long-fronted, black and white timbered house owned in the mid-seventeenth century by a descendant of a prince of Powys and member of the royal court of Charles I. Plas Penmynydd on Anglesey was once the home of the Tudor ancestors of Henry VII, while Plas Newydd, the home of the Marquis of Anglesey, has been in the care of the National Trust since 1976. The Trust is also responsible for Erddig Hall near Wrexham, built for Joshua Edisbury in 1683 and the home of Philip Yorke in the eighteenth century.

Those classes in Welsh society below the gentry possessed few material comforts. The yeoman class was reasonably well housed, clothed and fed, many were literate, and a few could afford to send their sons to grammar schools and universities. They served as local administrators and parish officials. Husbandmen generally farmed on a small scale and close to the breadline, some acquiring a second part-time craft occupation in order to survive. Similarly, many rural craftsmen – such as saddlers, coopers and turners – grew crops and kept livestock. A fair proportion of these were literate and cultured. About one-third of the population in the late Stuart period were labourers, landless, mobile, unskilled, who received a pittance for long hours of drudgery, and lived in tiny hovels. Substantial numbers of paupers lay at the foot of the social pyramid, rigidly divided into the deserving and undeserving poor. The former – the old, orphans, the sick and the disabled – received some relief from the parish, the Church and benevolent gentry. The latter – thriftless vagrants, rogues and vagabonds – were arrested, whipped, punished in the houses of correction and sent back to their native parishes.

# 6

# Methodism and Radicalism

## The Welsh Church

Many of the clergy of the early eighteenth century in Wales were poor and ignorant. In many cases country squires had replaced parish priests as recipients of tithes; this had occurred in as many as 250 of the 300 parishes in the diocese of St Davids. The salaries paid to clergymen were consequently very low, and many were compelled to hold more than one living. The plight of curates was even worse, many sharing the abysmal standard of living of their poorest parishioners. Few clergymen had received a university education. Many of the bishops who were appointed to the poverty-stricken Welsh sees remained non-resident, regarding their dioceses as short-term stepping stones to more lucrative preferments in England, and many resorted to practices such as nepotism. All too often such abuses were accepted as a fact of life. The Church remained very much a medieval institution lacking both the means and the will to reform itself. Not a single bishop able to preach in Welsh was appointed to a Welsh see between 1713 and 1870.

## Welsh printed books

In spite of poor spiritual leadership, the number of printed books in Wales multiplied dramatically during the two generations after the Restoration. At least 545 Welsh books were published between 1660 and 1730, a fivefold increase on the total which had appeared between 1546 and 1660. This dramatic transformation was brought about by the philanthropic work of the Welsh Trust, the passage of the Toleration Act of 1689, the lapsing of the Licensing Act in 1695 (which had imposed censorship), the formation of the Society for Promoting Christian Knowledge in 1699, and the emergence of the first printing presses in Wales – at Trefhedyn in Cardiganshire in 1718 and Carmarthen in 1721. Many of the works produced were translations of English best sellers – such as Bayly's *Practise of Piety* and Allestree's *Whole Duty of Man* – which aimed to instil the basic tenets of Protestantism by encouraging private worship and prayers within the family unit. Six major editions of the Bible appeared during the same period, and the Bible became a highly prized family heirloom especially among literate farmers, merchants and craftsmen. Cheap editions of the Welsh Prayer Book and of catechisms and primers abounded. Reading was largely an oral activity practised in informal reading groups around the family hearth.

## *The Welsh Trust*

The appearance of printed books stimulated an awareness of the need for literacy and education. The foundations of a state system of education had been laid during the years of the Commonwealth. The work was extended by the efforts of the Welsh Trust, a charitable body founded in 1674 by an ejected minister, Thomas Gouge, who became much interested in the plight of Wales and enlisted London gentlemen and merchants, and some in Wales, to contribute substantial sums of money to establish English schools in Wales and to publish Welsh books. Gouge was assisted by Charles Edwards and Stephen Hughes who won the support of all denominations, Anglicans and Dissenters alike, for the venture. By 1675, 2,225 children were being taught to read, write and prepare accounts in English in 87 schools in the market towns of Wales which were to be 'little garrisons against Popery'. Of all the Welsh counties Merioneth alone had no school, although there was a heavy

preponderance in south Wales and the borders. These efforts were
paralleled by the distribution of Welsh books; more than 5,000 were
circulated in 1678 alone, much of this pious literature suitable for
the family household. But these efforts aroused much enmity and
resentment in Wales, and Gouge's death in 1681 spelled the death-
knell of a laudable movement.

## The SPCK

In March 1699 a new educational initiative was launched under the
auspices of the Society for Promoting Christian Knowledge, an
initiative which was warmly welcomed in Wales as a means of
eliminating the 'reigning diseases' of ignorance and poverty. Poor
children were again taught the three Rs in a large number of charity
schools established throughout Wales, some sixty-eight by 1714.
Older pupils also received more practical training in farming,
seamanship, knitting, weaving and spinning. The Bible, Prayer Book
and devotional works again formed the backbone of the teaching.
Impoverished incumbents and curates only too readily served as
schoolteachers, while many local baronets and gentlemen provided
financial support, foremost among them Sir John Philipps of Picton
Castle in Pembrokeshire.

Unlike the Welsh Trust, the SPCK permitted the use of Welsh
alongside English in the schools, at least in north Wales. The Society
was also responsible for the publication of a new edition of the Bible
in Welsh, the distribution of thousands of religious books and tracts
in Welsh and English, and the establishment of a number of libraries
including major centres at Carmarthen, Cowbridge, Bangor and St
Asaph, at each of which books to the value of £60 were provided.
Numerous small local libraries were also established. Ninety-six
schools were opened in all in Wales.

But a period of alarming decline began with the accession of the
Hanoverians in 1714. The bitter controversies which stemmed from
the passage of the Schism Act in the same year meant the loss of
much Dissenter support. The schools were widely condemned as

seminaries of Jacobitism. They had prospered best in the Anglicized market towns of Wales where a hard core of relatively well-to-do merchants, traders and craftsmen existed, convinced of the value of literacy and possessing the means and the motivation to send their children to day schools. Small farmers and labourers required their children to assist at home, particularly at harvest-time, and were reluctant to spare them. The widespread use of English in the schools in south Wales further alienated many parents and schoolmasters alike.

## *Griffith Jones's circulating schools*

A scheme first launched in 1731 became one of the major success stories of Welsh history. Griffith Jones, a native of Penboyr in Carmarthenshire, became the incumbent of Llandeilo Abercywyn in 1711. Five years later he was presented to the living of Llanddowror by Sir John Philipps whose sister he married. The death of a large number of his parishioners from a typhus epidemic between 1727 and 1731 vexed him greatly. In the latter year, convinced that preaching alone was inadequate as a means of salvation, he appealed to the SPCK for a stock of some forty to fifty Welsh Bibles with which he planned to teach his adult parishioners to read. He devised a scheme of employing itinerant ministers because of the difficulties of maintaining a school in each parish. The number of schools multiplied dramatically after 1737. Many parish clergy held the schools or else itinerant teachers gave classes within the parish church for a period of about three to four months, usually during the autumn and winter when farming families had more leisure. Adults and children were invited to attend the classes which aimed to do no more than teach them to read Welsh by using the Bible and the Catechism as the basic textbooks. Additional evening classes were held to enable tenants, craftsmen, labourers and farm servants to attend after a day's work. At Llanddowror Jones himself supervised the training of his teachers, relying upon the assistance of the SPCK and of a number of wealthy patrons to meet the considerable expense. Foremost among these was Madam Bevan of Laugharne. Subscribers to the schools received an annual report of numbers of schools and pupils under the title *Welch Piety*. These reports reveal that 158,237 pupils had been taught in 3,495 classes by the time of Jones's death in 1761. In all some 250,000 adults and children were taught to read by the circulating schools, more than half the population of Wales!

### Thomas Charles of Bala

Born in 1755 at Llanfihangel Abercywyn, Carmarthenshire, and educated at Llanddowror and Oxford. From 1778 to 1783 he served as an Anglican incumbent in Somerset, but then moved to Bala. He joined the Methodists in 1784 and devoted the rest of his life to furthering the cause. His educational work in establishing a successful Sunday School movement in north Wales convinced him of the importance of the Catechism and he published works such as *A Short Evangelical Catechism* (1801). He was an able defender and leader of the Methodists against the many attacks made from the standpoint of the Established Church. In a Biblical dictionary published in four volumes from 1805 to 1811 he presented new information about the history and geography of the Bible lands. Another major achievement was the standardization of the text of the first Welsh Bible to be published by the British and Foreign Bible Society. In 1806 there appeared under his editorship an edition of the New Testament prepared under the auspices of the SPCK. His final editorial feat was the Bible of 1814, an edition of great accuracy reflecting years of intensive study. He died in 1814.

The schools declined sharply after about 1780. Although Madam Bevan left £10,000 to maintain the schools upon her death in 1779, the money was not available until 1809 because her will was contested. Jones had aimed to employ religious instruction to save souls; his efforts also helped to preserve the Welsh language by acquainting much of the population of Wales with the standard literary language of the Bible. A substantial reading public was the result of his efforts, a public which consequently responded readily to the appeal of Methodism.

### *Thomas Charles and the Sunday Schools*

After Griffith Jones's death, Thomas Charles of Bala attempted to establish a similar system of circulating schools in north Wales. This eventually developed into the Sunday School movement which provided education and instruction for adults and children alike. These schools ensured that the Scriptures became part of the everyday speech of the Welsh, and provided a new stimulus to the spiritual and philosophical development of the nation. Ordinary people were encouraged to form and express opinions, to exercise their minds and to discuss thoughtfully amongst themselves. The Sunday Schools were a fillip and an inspiration to Methodism and Nonconformity in general in Wales.

*Capel Soar-y-Mynydd, near Llanddewibrefi, Dyfed,*
*a remote Calvinistic Methodist chapel built in 1828.*

## The Methodist Revival

The Methodist Revival represented the full coming of age of the Protestant Reformation in Wales, and the early Methodist leaders attempted to revive and reawaken the traditional Protestant philosophies. Howel Harris became the organizer of the Methodist movement in Wales, after his conversion in 1735. Although never permitted to take Anglican orders, Harris was an effective preacher, soon to be joined in his crusade by William Williams of Pantycelyn in Carmarthenshire, Daniel Rowland of Llangeitho in Cardiganshire and a host of others such as Howel Davies and Peter Williams. All had experienced a sweeping personal conversion and became convinced that they were part of God's plan to transform the course of Welsh history.

### Howel Harris

Born in 1714 at Trefeca in the parish of Talgarth, Breconshire. He served as a schoolmaster at Llangorse from 1732 to 1735 when he was converted by the preaching of the vicar of Talgarth. He himself began to evangelize in the neighbourhood, and entered St Mary Hall, Oxford, in the hope of taking holy orders, but left after a few days. He was refused ordination by the bishop on four occasions because of his preaching activities out of doors and in private houses. He came into contact with like-minded religious enthusiasts such as Daniel Rowland and William Williams (Pantycelyn) in Wales and George Whitefield and the Wesley brothers in England. Harris became the organizer of the Methodist Revival in Wales, the creator of the 'societies' and 'associations'. He remained anxious to keep the doors of Wales open for John Wesley, which was the root of a rift between himself and his fellow leaders resulting in 'The Great Schism' in their ranks. In 1754 he retired from his public role to Trefeca where he assembled a 'Family' of converts to live and work with him, and began a press in 1757. Three years later he became reconciled with his former friends and returned to the work of the Revival. He was not an outstanding preacher but possessed charisma, abounding energy and persuasiveness. He was a founder member of the Brecknockshire Agricultural Society in 1755 and served as a militia captain in charge of a company from 'the Family'. He kept detailed 'journals', wrote a few hymns and attempted an autobiography. He died in 1773.

The widespread success of their preaching conventions led to the growth of a network of small societies which met in private houses to discuss religion. What claimed their attention above all else was the state of the soul and spiritual progress of the individual member. Their methods and meetings were characterized by enthusiasm – frenzied, provocative emotional preaching, dancing and leaping around, simple lyrical songs. They felt that they had received a commission to proclaim Christ's message and to save souls everywhere. Many of the sermons were delivered out of doors in fairs, markets and churchyards, although they also preached in parish churches when no objection arose. Many Methodists, however, experienced their conversions within the 'societies' – small classes composed of some five to twelve members – which aimed to foster the individual's spiritual development, and where members were encouraged to confess their shame and sins, to give expression to their experiences and fears, and to seek comfort, grace and conversion. Many of the most important hymns of William Williams, Pantycelyn, are the products of profound personal experiences felt within these societies, and it was he above all who succeeded in expressing and conveying to posterity the vitality, energy and indeed ecstasy of the movement.

## Daniel Rowland

Born in 1713, the son of the incumbent of Nantcwnlle and Llangeitho, Cardiganshire. He was ordained in 1735 and served as a curate in the same parishes before being converted to Methodism after listening to a sermon by Griffith Jones. He met Howel Harris in 1737; together they assumed the leadership of the Methodist Revival, but later quarrelled and went their separate ways in 1752. He remained true to Whitefield's Calvinism rather than Wesley's Arminianism. He built a chapel at Llangeitho and led the revival which stemmed from that village in 1762. He was an excellent preacher whose sermons attracted thousands from all parts of Wales. He was the author of a number of Welsh books, and many of his sermons were published in two volumes in 1772 and 1775. He died in 1790.

The Methodists, appealing to the heart as well as to the head, won converts among the vast underprivileged masses, among the young, women and the very poor. But first and foremost Methodism was a movement of the 'middling sorts' in eighteenth-century Welsh society, farmers and craftsmen in particular, literate, sober, reasonably prosperous people, vocal and articulate in their opinions, ripe to respond. This contrasts starkly with John Wesley's appeal amongst the poor in England. Before the 1760s Methodism was most successful in south Wales where there persisted a powerful tradition of Dissent and of theological debate and a greater receptivity to external influences. A quarrel between Harris and the other leaders in 1752 led to a split and to a weakening in support until the dispute was resolved in 1763. Thereafter remarkable successes were experienced in the virgin territory of the north, marked by a second wave of revivalism with Pantycelyn's hymns at its centre. The techniques of the Methodists were consciously emulated by other Dissenting sects such as the Baptists and the Independents who also grew dramatically towards the end of the century.

## William Williams, Pantycelyn

Born in 1717 at Cefn-coed, Llanfair-ar-y-bryn, Carmarthenshire. His father was a farmer and an elder of Cefnarthen Independent Church. He was educated locally and at Chancefield Nonconformist Academy near Talgarth, Breconshire. Abandoning plans to become a physician, in 1737 he was converted by the preaching of Howel Harris at Talgarth. In 1740 he took Deacon's orders and became curate to Theophilus Evans at Llanwrtyd, Llanfihangel Abergwesyn and Llanddewi Abergwesyn, Breconshire. His extraparochial Methodist activities, however, meant that he was refused priest's orders in 1743. He devoted the rest of his life to the Methodist movement as an itinerant preacher and a founder and overseer of Methodist societies. In 1748 he married and settled at Pantycelyn. His first publication was *Aleluia* (1744), the first collection of a long stream of hymns which established him as the most important hymnwriter in Welsh history. His work conveys religious passion with a rare immediacy and symbolic richness although it is uneven in quality and often inaccurate in its use of language. He also wrote a number of important religious poems and some thirty elegies upon the deaths of fellow Methodists, in addition to distinguished prose works which aimed to encourage the spiritual growth of the converts of the Methodist Revival. In all he published some ninety books and pamphlets. He died in 1791.

Methodism remained within the Anglican Church until 1811 when the Welsh Calvinistic connection was set up. It was estimated in 1816 that there were 343 Methodist causes in Wales; it was by far the largest non-Anglican body and one which enjoyed an influence far greater than its numbers. A religious revolution had taken place.

Why did the Welsh Methodists enjoy such overwhelming success? Their methods were novel, exciting, dramatic and far-reaching, enabling them to penetrate deep into Welsh society. The partial decay of ancient communities and old semi-pagan forms of popular culture had left something of a vacuum at a time when the individual's sense of his own personality was evolving. Methodism provided at the same time both joy and drama and also a sense of order and discipline and a tangible niche for the individual within a society in turmoil. Moreover, the massive force of streamlined, well-organized Anglicanism which stunted the growth of Dissent and Methodism in England was a much more feeble rival in Wales, where the Church was impoverished and archaic, incapable of providing adequate teaching or suitable services. To some extent Methodism in Wales was seen as a means of protesting against the traditional dominance of squire and parson. Wales lacked many of the attractions which early eighteenth-century England offered: the potential of an elaborate aristocratic existence, large-scale commerce, business and industry, and a lively cultural or political life. Methodism was thus able to provide an excitement which ensured its success in Wales.

## Ann Griffiths

Born in 1776 at Dolwar Fach in Llanfihangel-yng-Ngwynfa in Montgomeryshire. In 1796 she experienced a religious conversion, and became a member of the Methodist fellowship at Pontrobert. Subsequently she devoted her life completely to God and the Methodist cause, and Dolwar Fach became a centre of Methodist preaching.

She is today remembered for her letters and hymns. The former vividly reflect the atmosphere of the Methodist meetings, while the latter, of which seventy-four survive, convey her personal, intense, spiritual experiences. She also possessed much ability as a poet, employing rhythmic, melodious language in the Calvinistic Methodist tradition. She died in 1805 shortly after the birth of a daughter.

The movement transformed the lives of numerous individuals and eventually provided a stimulus to other Nonconformist denominations. It was to lead to a revitalizing of both the Church and Nonconformity. The traditional Puritan virtues – such as integrity, thrift, honesty and temperance – were reinforced by the new earnestness and by the emphasis placed on sin and evil. The Methodists also launched an assault on the joy which stemmed from the traditional folk practices of Welsh communities. In politics their impact, too, was negative; their basic doctrine was acceptance of one's lot in life, quiescence and non-involvement, and they urged their followers to steer clear of Radical movements. Yet they exerted a profound and far-reaching influence on the religious, philosophical, literary and social life of Wales. The chapel was to become the focal point of social life and was to dominate the people's activities in the rural areas and new industrial districts alike, to act as 'an opiate to the suffering produced by the Industrial Revolution'.

## Literature and the Eisteddfod

Wales saw a remarkable literary renaissance in the eighteenth century. Ellis Wynne's *Bardd Cwsc* published in 1703 embodied the

Puritan virtues in its virulent condemnation of vice and licentiousness, but its style and the imagery it contains are outstanding. The origins of the revival were antiquarian. *Archaeologia Britannica* (1707), the work of Edward Lhuyd, the Keeper of the Ashmolean Museum at Oxford, examined the origins of the Welsh language and was to influence all subsequent Celtic studies. Theophilus Evans's approach, although he attempted to emulate Lhuyd, was far from scholarly in his account of Welsh history in *Drych y Prif Oesoedd* (1716). But the impact of this work was considerable for to most literate Welshmen his legendary account was their sole concept of their nation's history. One of Wales's foremost poets, Goronwy Owen, wrote in the traditional Welsh bardic forms with great accuracy and restrained language, a reflection of the eighteenth-century Augustan school in English literature. The study of Welsh literature was fostered by the Honourable Society of Cymmrodorion founded in 1751 and the Gwyneddigion Society formed in 1771 by London Welshmen. The history and the scenery of Wales now absorbed the attention of many English writers on a scale hitherto unknown, and were reflected in a rich array of topographical literature. The growing interest in Welsh antiquities and the impact of the Romantic Movement brought about the revival of the eisteddfod, unheard of since the 1560s. Its foremost sponsors were Thomas Jones of Corwen and Iolo Morganwg, creator of the *gorsedd* ceremony and hugely successful forger of the poetry of Dafydd ap Gwilym.

## Iolo Morganwg

Born Edward Williams in 1747 at Llancarfan, Glamorgan. He earned his living as a stonemason. As a young man he was influenced by a number of lexicographers and poets and by the cultural and antiquarian revival in Wales. He himself became a poet in Welsh and English, a collector and copyist of manuscripts and an antiquary. He became an active member of the Gwyneddigion Society in London in the 1770s, he frequented Radical circles and in 1802 he helped to found the Unitarian Society in south Wales. He suffered a large number of business failures and was declared a bankrupt. It was he who introduced the *Gorsedd*, his own invention, as a preliminary to the Eisteddfod held at the Ivy Bush Tavern in Carmarthen in 1819.

In 1789 he published a volume of poetry which he claimed was the work of Dafydd ap Gwilym, but which was in fact his own. He also published English poetry, a large number of hymns, a treatise on Welsh metrics and much miscellaneous prose and verse, most of which appeared after his death. He made a major contribution to our understanding of the history and literature of Glamorgan. But he did have a fertile imagination and was prepared to exercise his great gifts to falsify the sources of Welsh history and mislead contemporaries. He was eventually exposed as a forger by the researches of Griffith John Williams. Iolo's last years were spent preparing literary and historical material for the press. He died at Flemingstone in the Vale of Glamorgan in 1826.

## Political life

The parliamentary representation of Wales came to be dominated by a highly select and affluent group of county families who went from strength to strength both economically and politically. Throughout the eighteenth century a narrow circle of famous county families represented Wales at Westminster such as the Williams-Wynn family, the Morgans of Tredegar, the Mansels of Margam, the Vaughans of Golden Grove and the Bulkeleys of Baron Hill. They came to regard the county seats as their own property, a reflection of their undisputed economic prosperity, bringing wide-ranging prestige and power. Constituencies were regarded as family heirlooms to be bequeathed from one generation to the next. Such representatives, convinced of the success and value of the Union of 1536, identified themselves closely with England, and grew to venerate the English constitution which they considered durable, stable and just, a pattern of perfection. The protection of property became their primary concern.

The small, inadequate, Welsh electorate – no more than 25,000 men, some four per cent of the population – was incapable of mounting an effective challenge to this hegemony; politics was a matter for indifference. Voting for one's political master was considered an act of homage as much in the new industrial society as in long-standing rural communities. Such an attitude was strengthened by the teaching of the circulating schools and the Methodist societies. In any case, contested elections were extremely rare events in both county and borough constituencies, partly because the costs involved were considerable. The few elections which did occur were characterized by family feuds, petty intrigues and a wide range of corrupt malpractices. Election officials readily displayed blatant partisanship and often engaged in unfair dealings.

The record of the Welsh MPs at Westminster at this time was undistinguished. Party labels largely lacked meaning, generally reflecting family tradition and rivalries rather than policy, and no distinct Welsh issues emerged in political life. Many members rarely attended debates, preferring to channel their energies into ensuring preferment for members of their families and servants. Some totally lacked interest in national politics, viewing national political leaders with a mixture of suspicion and contempt.

### Williams-Wynn family

Of Wynnstay, Ruabon, Denbighshire. They became the greatest landed family in Wales, owning by the nineteenth century 150,000 acres in Denbighshire, Merioneth and Montgomeryshire. William Williams (1634–1700) became Speaker of the House of Commons and Attorney-General, and purchased the Llanforda estate near Oswestry. Successive members of the family acquired by marriage the Glascoed estate, the Plas-y-Ward estate, the Gwydir estate, the Wynnstay estate, the Llwydiarth estate and the Mathafarn estate. A long succession of Wynns represented Denbighshire in Parliament from 1716 to 1885 until the seventh baronet was defeated by George Osborne Morgan in the latter year. Charles Williams Wynn, one of the few Welshmen to sit in the Cabinet in the nineteenth century, also represented Montgomeryshire from 1799 to 1850. So extensive were the lands they built up that members of the family became known as the 'uncrowned kings of north Wales'. Upon the death of the tenth baronet in 1951 the mansion at Glanllyn near Bala became (and remains to this day) a centre for *Urdd Gobaith Cymru*. Wynnstay is now the home of Lindisfarne College.

## Jacobitism

Few in Wales protested against the accession of George I in 1714. Die-hard Jacobites, supporters of the right to the throne of England of the Catholic Stuarts, included Sir Watkin Williams-Wynn of Wynnstay, Lord Bulkeley and Lewis Pryse of Gogerddan. Most Dissenters rejoiced at the Hanoverian succession, while of the 300 clergymen who had refused to swear allegiance to William and Mary, only eighteen came from Wales. Very few Welsh adherents had followed James II into exile, but there is evidence of Jacobite clubs in Cardiganshire and Montgomeryshire. A Jacobite society in south-west Wales known as the Sea Serjeants was revived in 1725, while a similar society was active in Anglesey in the 1730s, and a secret Jacobite club called the Circle of the White Rose met at Wrexham under the leadership of Sir Watkin Williams-Wynn. But no effort was made to achieve concerted action or to create a national body. A minor disturbance in Wrexham accompanied the rebellion of 1715, and a Jacobite mob armed with cudgels caused some alarm in Pembrokeshire, but Wales generally was peaceable and law-abiding. Similarly, when the 1745 Rebellion broke out, very little support came from Wales. The mission of the young soldier, Henry Lloyd of Cwmbychan in Merioneth, to rouse north Wales to the Young Pretender's cause proved futile. Welsh activities displayed a complete lack of planning and foresight. Indeed, Jacobitism was primarily a social movement in Wales, the preserve of a small select group of the county gentry, unrealistic and over-optimistic. Most of the Welsh squirearchy readily transferred their loyalty to the House of Hanover, revelling in their association with the throne and in the prospects for political prizes and self-advancement through contacts at court and with active politicians. Many great Welsh families – Chirk, Glynllifon, Margam and Mostyn among them – were implacably hostile to the Jacobite cause, while Williams-Wynn died in 1749.

## *The new Radicalism*

But the changes of the second half of the eighteenth century (the Age of Rationalism) did create a new climate in Wales which was to prove a congenial breeding ground for radical ideas. This was the age of the Enlightenment and of philosophers such as Voltaire, Diderot, Rousseau and Montesquieu. Their works were read widely by Welsh students in the Nonconformist academies, where they were encouraged to question concepts such as Biblical truth and divine intervention. By the 1740s the Arminian tenets had taken root in the area between the Rivers Aeron and Teifi in Cardiganshire. 'Heretical' ideas spread throughout much of Wales, the products of the Arminians, Arians, Unitarians and Deists.

These questioning attitudes were given impetus by the American War of Independence. In 1776 the famous Declaration of Independence was published and coincided with the appearance of the seminal work *Observations on the Nature of Civil Liberty* by Dr Richard Price, a Radical philosopher. This pamphlet soon sold 60,000 copies and ran to twelve editions by the end of the year. Price claimed that each community had the right to govern itself, that MPs were simply the trustees of their constituents, responsible for executing their electors' wishes, and that the denial of this responsibility constituted treason. His arguments influenced the outlook of the American colonists. Another Welshman, David Williams, a native of Caerphilly and a pure Deist, was also of importance by the 1780s for his trenchant and outspoken essays on education, religious freedom and the franchise. His most influential publication was *Letters on Political Liberty* which appeared in 1782 and propounded advanced political ideas which anticipated the demands of the Chartists. The works of Price and Williams were read by only a tiny fraction of the Welsh population, but political pamphlets began to be issued in Welsh from the 1770s, and ballad-writers openly voiced criticism of the government during the American war and advocated democratic principles.

## Richard Price

Born at Llangeinor, Glamorgan, in 1723, he was educated at a number of the dissenting academies, and became a family chaplain to George Streatfield at Stoke Newington. Streatfield's death in 1757 led him to become a minister at a number of London meeting-houses. At the same time he published a series of substantial essays on theology and divinity, and acquired an expertise on actuarial and demographic matters, influencing the financial policies of Shelburne and William Pitt.

His *Observations on the Nature of Civil Liberty* (1776) and other pamphlets ensured that his fame became more widespread. He never wavered from his opinion that the American colonies had an absolute right to oppose the demands of the British Parliament, an attitude which earned him much opprobrium and yet much respect for raising the level of debate. He was the recipient of a number of honours in England and America, but refused an invitation to become an American citizen. He is now best remembered for his *A Discourse ...* (1789), which reveals his ecstatic enthusiam for the opening events of the French Revolution. He died in 1791.

Meanwhile, demands for parliamentary reform – universal suffrage, annual parliaments and equal electoral districts – began to absorb the attention of Welsh Nonconformists, who as a group were relatively prosperous and perhaps the best educated in Welsh society. Nonconformists were still subject to some disabilities: forced to defend the religious liberty of the individual against the State, they soon began to defend the political liberty of the individual. But it cannot be denied that, at the outbreak of the French Revolution, only a small minority of the Welsh embraced democratic ideas, in the main only literate and articulate Dissenters, lively, aware, middling sorts. As for the ordinary people, the Church, the Methodists and the schoolmasters ensured they knew nothing of their political rights and of their right to shape their own destiny.

## The French Revolution

Richard Price welcomed the revolution as the beginning of an improvement in the history of mankind. In his sermon, *A Discourse on the Love of our Country*, which he preached on 4 November 1789, he maintained that sovereignty resided in the people to whom the king was responsible, a line of argument which drew from Burke his *Reflections on the Revolution in France*. There was further sympathy for the Revolution from other London Welshmen who had fostered closer links with their Welsh homeland and from some Nonconformist ministers in south Wales. Morgan John Rhys, a Baptist minister from Glamorgan, went to Paris in 1791 to distribute bibles, returned home and edited five numbers of *Cylch-grawn Cynmraeg* ('Welsh Journal'), the first Welsh periodical to discuss religious and political themes, and attempted to establish political clubs in south Wales. The Unitarian minister Thomas Evans (Tomos Glyn Cothi) published three numbers of *The Miscellaneous Repository or Y Drysorfa Gymmysgedig* in 1795, and was imprisoned in 1801 perhaps for singing seditious songs. John Jones (Jac Glan-y-gors) published two important pamphlets in Welsh in 1795 and 1797, both largely derived from Tom Paine's *The Rights of Man*. Such men were basically pamphleteers, anxious to oppose tyranny and oppression but with no planned campaign of reform. Most Welshmen were loyal to the monarchy.

When the French landed at Carreg Wastad in Pembrokeshire on 22 February 1797 as part of a plan for the invasion of Ireland, it led to panic and alarm in south-west Wales, increased by rumours of local Dissenter involvement. In the event the 'invasion' was a fiasco. Patriotic fervour subsequently grew in Wales against the Napoleonic menace, a fervour which was reinforced by the excesses of the Revolution, especially the attacks upon Christianity, and by the hardships of war and war taxation.

### Jemima Nicholas

A heroine who, according to tradition, helped to defeat the French invasion in 1797. A French expeditionary force, led by an American named Tate, had been sent up the Bristol Channel to start a peasants' revolt in England. The winds compelled the force to land on the Welsh coast where, after a few days of looting, the French surrendered to the Castlemartin Yeomanry under Lord Cawdor. Tradition attributes their capture to a crowd of local women led by Jemima Nicholas, dressed in red shawls and tall, black hats, and whom, it is claimed, the French mistook for soldiery. She was reputed to have captured single-handed a number of Frenchmen by using a pitchfork. She died in 1832.

Yet a legacy remained of Welsh Radical grievances: the oppression of the political system, the payment of the tithe (especially resented by the growing number of Nonconformists), the operation of the legal system (considered to be the preserve of the privileged classes) and economic injustice, felt all the more sharply because of industrial changes and the economic effects of the French Wars on the price of corn, the shortage of bread, inflation and low wages. These Radical grievances were repressed by the continuing political and economic stranglehold of the 'Great Leviathans' on Wales, the influences of the Church and of Methodism, and by repressive action and legislation on the part of the government during the French Wars. Privilege and property still held sway in 1815, but the seeds of the Radical struggle for freedom and justice had at least been sown in Wales, and were soon to come to fruition in the powerful alliance of Radical Nonconformity and an articulate, politically conscious working class in the nineteenth century.

# 7

# The Agrarian and Industrial Revolutions

## Welsh agriculture

Welsh agriculture remained primitive well into the nineteenth century; holdings were generally small, and farming techniques static, bequeathed from one generation to the next. Most of the land was in the occupation of small tenant farmers who paid an annual rent. Ploughing was inefficient, the use of root crops largely unknown, crop rotation rarely practised, and lime used indiscriminately as the sole means of fertilization. Oats and barley provided the staple diet. Inevitably, the damp climate and the hilly terrain meant that pastoralism predominated over tillage. The rearing of sheep and cattle sustained a range of subsidiary industries vital to the Welsh economy: a buoyant trade in woollen goods, the spinning of wool into yarn (a cottage industry admirably suited to the womenfolk of farming communities) and the sale of butter and cheese at markets in London, Bristol and the border areas. Cattle were raised primarily as a source of meat for London and other centres in England, and drovers remained prestigious members of the community until the advent of railways, although they were often unpopular for cheating the peasants.

## The Agrarian Revolution

The eighteenth century had seen far-reaching and rapid changes in English agricultural techniques, encouraged by the need to satisfy an increasingly urbanized, industrialized and growing population. Wales inevitably lagged far behind advanced major arable areas such as East Anglia, although Breconshire was the home of one of the earliest agricultural societies in Britain in 1755. The new ideas were slow to make any impact on Wales where roads were narrow and poorly maintained, the new English farming manuals rarely read, the great landowners often absent, and the yeoman class was lacking in capital and initiative.

A change did occur, however, during the Napoleonic Wars (1793–1815) which saw rampant inflation in Wales as elsewhere, and a truly massive increase in the price of grain. Welsh farmers, pressed to increase their output of foodstuffs, brought more and more land under the plough, including grassland, marginal land and much hilly terrain. Enclosure of common and waste land was practised on a large scale. Secondly, pioneers such as Arthur Young, Sir John Sinclair and William Marshall brought the new agricultural techniques to Wales. Some of the great landowners, anxious to maximize profits, now displayed intense interest in the new methods. By the end of the wars all parts of Wales had local or county agricultural societies. Above all, the improvement of grassland was encouraged, in terms of pasture quality and breeding stock. Rather than practising the mass slaughter of cattle in the autumn on All Saints' Day because of the lack of fodder in the winter, farmers kept them alive throughout the year and the population enjoyed fresh rather than salted meat which had previously led to widespread malnutrition. Crop rotations began to be introduced in the arable areas following successful patterns practised in Norfolk where a turnips, oats, clover and wheat pattern was generally exercised. Output was thus increased, production costs lowered and profits maximized. Innovation and experimentation took pride of place, not least in the scientific breeding of cattle and sheep.

Even so Wales lagged behind much of England in these advances. Inevitably, it was the landed gentry and the farmers of the better land who had most to gain; lack of capital restricted the efforts of small farmers. A survey of 1801 reveals that oats remained the predominant crop in much of Wales; barley had assumed first place only in south Pembrokeshire, Gower and the Vale of Clwyd, and wheat only in eastern Monmouthshire, the Vale of Glamorgan and the lowland valleys of the Severn, Wye and Usk. Arthur Young had expressed amazement at the primitive state of Glamorgan agriculture in the 1760s and 1770s. Although much improvement occurred within the next forty years, it was not uniform and it took place relatively late and slowly.

## Transport in rural areas

Improvements in communications largely stemmed from industrial developments, but they also facilitated agricultural changes. From the 1790s onwards, canals provided links between some of the lowland agricultural areas and the manufacturing centres and major ports. But most agricultural produce was carried by road. From 1555 parishes were responsible for maintaining roads, and from 1675 they were permitted to erect toll-gates to meet these expenses. From about 1750 companies called turnpike trusts were set up and secured government consent to build new roads or improve existing ones. To raise the money, the trusts issued road bonds on which they paid interest and, to reimburse themselves, erected more toll-gates at which travellers on horseback or in carriages were required to pay tolls. The trusts produced a road network favourably received by contemporary commentators, links with England were increased, especially with major border market towns, trade was promoted and the channels of communication improved, especially with the completion of the Irish mail road through Carmarthen in 1787. Many bridges were constructed in the wake of the roads, such as the notable bridge at Pontypridd built by William Edwards. But there is evidence that some trusts mismanaged the roads in their care and increased the number of gates to such an extent that they became a burden on agriculture and fostered rural discontent.

## Enclosures

The enclosing of open fields and waste land enabled foodstuffs to be produced in greatly increased quantities. In Wales land along the mountainsides, previously cultivated by small farmers on their own initiative, was enclosed on a large scale. The enclosure of waste by private act of Parliament was possible from the early eighteenth century. Many such acts were passed relating to Wales before 1793, but between 1793 and 1815 seventy-six such acts were introduced covering some 200,000 acres, about one-eighth of the total common and waste land. The commissioners named in the act (in practice often the stewards of the larger estates) apportioned the common and tended to favour the large landowners at the expense of the 'squatters', who had to have occupied their holdings for twenty-one years to have a legal right of ownership. Ownership disputes were common in the moorlands and local opposition to enclosure could be intense; riots occurred at Llanddeiniolen in Caernarfonshire in 1809 and on Mynydd Bach in Cardiganshire in 1812, but violent reactions of such intensity were rare. Three kinds of land were liable to enclosure: upland moors, coastal waste and low-lying marsh and valley land. Large tracts of the Welsh countryside were thus modified: new farmsteads were constructed, new hedges and fences built, and new access roads created. The prevention of the aimless roaming of animals facilitated scientific breeding. But a price had to be paid: many small farmers and tenants simply could not absorb the costs of enclosure and of hedging their lands and some were pressurized into migrating to the new industrial regions. Some were left with insufficient land to support their cattle, and considerable hardship resulted.

## Rural discontent

During the French Wars in particular, the small-scale farmer was hard hit: grazing rights were forfeited, rents rose, corn was scarce and expensive, and a series of wet, poor harvests occurred between

1795 and 1800 and again between 1808 and 1812. Moreover, a dramatic acceleration occurred in the rate of population increase, further straining the already overstretched resources of the Welsh countryside. Abject poverty was the result, with whole districts on the brink of famine, a state of affairs which prevailed until the end of the Hungry Forties. Droves of Welsh farmers had to sell up, and many were ruined by the collapse of rural banks in the 1820s. Short-term leases were often introduced, rack-renting was common, and the fear of eviction or displacement ever present. After the end of the war in 1815, the prices of agricultural commodities fell, some industrial workers returned to their native countryside to escape the effects of industrial depression, new machinery was more widely used, displacing agricultural labourers, taxes were high and resentment was widespread. A clear-cut class conflict now existed in the Welsh countryside, a basic cleavage between the opulent, largely non-resident, Anglicized and Anglican gentry and the poverty-striken, Nonconformist and Welsh-speaking peasantry. The Poor Law Amendment Act of 1834 abolished outdoor relief and, by creating the workhouses, imposed a much harsher code upon the able-bodied pauper. Two years later, the enforcement of a compulsory commutation of tithes, often in lay hands by this time, provoked a furious response from Welsh Nonconformists.

## The Rebecca Riots

Serious civil unrest broke out in the countryside of south-west Wales in 1839. There were many reasons for this, but the most tangible and visible symbols of the discontent were the toll-gates of the turnpike roads which had become too numerous and at which tolls were excessive. The tolls on lime were especially unpopular. New gates were constantly being erected by the trusts to avoid bankruptcy, and some towns such as Carmarthen were surrounded by toll-gates. The burning of the new workhouse at Narberth in January 1839 was followed in May by the destruction of a new gate at Efailwen on the borders of Carmarthenshire and Pembrokeshire. The same rebuilt gate was again destroyed a few weeks later, when some 400 people dressed in women's clothes drove away a group of specially sworn constables. Their leader – reputedly Thomas Rees (Twm Carnabwth) – had disguised himself, it is claimed, in the clothes of a local woman named Rebecca.

Peace then returned to the Welsh countryside for three and a half years. But without warning, in the winter of 1842, a new gate at St Clears was destroyed, an outbreak of violence which soon spilled over from Carmarthenshire and Pembrokeshire into south Cardiganshire and west Glamorgan, even into Radnorshire. In June 1843 the workhouse at Carmarthen was ransacked by a large crowd of more than 2,000. The destruction continued unabated although large contingents of special constables, London policemen and troops were dispatched to Wales. The death of an aged female gatekeeper in the autumn of 1843 deprived the movement of much popular sympathy and support, and it came to an end as suddenly as it had begun.

Some rioters served terms of imprisonment and a few were transported to Van Diemen's Land. In 1843 the government had set up a Commission of Enquiry to explore the causes of the riots. By an act of 1844 all the trusts within each shire in south Wales were amalgamated, the tolls on lime reduced by half, the pattern of payment simplified, and the debts of the older trusts liquidated. Rebecca had indeed won a substantial victory.

## The 'Land Question'

Economic conditions in rural Wales improved dramatically in the 1850s when the growth in the industrial population led to an increased demand for farm produce. The sudden penetration of the railways into remote rural areas gave Welsh farmers direct, rapid access to distant markets for the first time, rendering profitable the sale of fresh milk. The arrival of the railways also facilitated the migration of the surplus population of the Welsh countryside to the industrial areas.

In spite of the new-found prosperity, problems remained: geographical isolation, small-scale working and an unfriendly environment. Above all, a yawning gulf had opened up between the Nonconformist tenant farmers and the Anglicized landowners, staunch members of the Established Church, many of whom still viewed their estates as, first and foremost, sources of revenue, paying but little heed to the problems of their tenantry. They often employed English and Scottish land agents simply because they were prepared to be unsentimental, even ruthless, in the levying of extortionate rents and in the eviction of tenants who failed to pay or who voted against the political interest of their landlords. Here lay the crux of the 'Land Question' in late nineteenth-century Wales.

## Emigration

One escape route from the woes of rural poverty in the nineteenth century lay in emigration overseas. Indeed, a steady stream of Welsh people left for America throughout the century. In 1796 Morgan John Rhys purchased land in western Pennsylvania for the founding of the Cambrian Company at Philadelphia, a colony of Welsh people with Welsh as its official language. His scheme stood no chance of success for it ran contrary to the policy of the United States government of welding immigrants into a single nationality. Groups of Welsh families left for South Africa in 1820 and Brazil in 1850. In the 1850s, Samuel Roberts of Llanbrynmair purchased 100,000 acres of land in eastern Tennessee to establish a colony of Welsh settlers, but the impact of the American Civil War forced most of them to return home within ten years. In July 1865, a group of 150 Welsh people, under the leadership of Michael D. Jones, landed at the Chubut Valley on the eastern coast of Patagonia. Aided by the Argentinian government and the example of local Indian tribes, the colony overcame great privation and is still in existence to some extent today.

The depression which hit Welsh agriculture in the 1870s encouraged even more widespread emigration to Australia, Canada and the United States, closely paralleled by large numbers of emigrants from the industrial areas of Wales to the mines and ironworks of the United States, a migration stimulated by the impact of the infamous McKinley tariff on the Welsh tinplate industry. Meanwhile, in 1869, John Hughes, a native of Merthyr Tydfil who had worked at the Cyfarthfa ironworks, emigrated to Russia and, at the invitation of the Russian government, formed the New Russia Company for the development of the iron and steel industries in the country. The town which grew up around his foundries and to which many Welsh people emigrated became known as Yuzovka.

## Welsh industry

The accelerating pace of industrial change was a striking feature of the eighteenth-century Welsh economy which became more productive and more diversified than ever before. A number of factors came together to create the Welsh industrial revolution: the emergence of new inventions which increased the rate of production and lowered labour costs; the inflow of substantial capital, generally provided by English adventurers; and the impact of war, which demanded new inventions and stimulated new demands for iron, copper, lead, tinplate and coal. As we have seen, before about 1750 industrial enterprises in Wales had been localized, small-scale affairs, employing much of their labour force on a part-time or seasonal basis. All this was soon to change. In Anglesey the Parys and Mona copper mines, owned by Thomas Williams, the 'copper king', employed 1,200 men and enabled Williams to dictate the market price of the metal between 1787 and 1792. He set up smelting works at Amlwch and near Swansea, and acquired a large fleet of ships. The slate quarries of Gwynedd were greatly extended by Richard Pennant, Lord Penrhyn. The establishment of the Holywell copper and brass works gave a new lease of life to an old-established industrial development in north-east Wales. Tinplate manufacture flourished at Pontypool, and pottery at Ewenny, Swansea and Nantgarw.

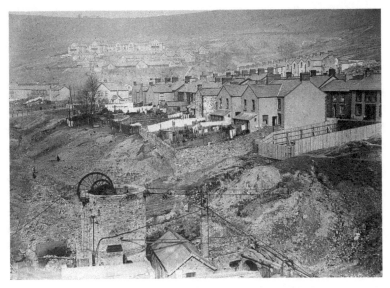

*Glamorgan Colliery. Llwynypia, Rhondda, Mid Glamorgan.*

## *The iron industry*

John Wilkinson organized the Bersham ironworks in north-east Wales, while in the south two areas became heavily industrialized: the Swansea-Neath district, noted for its copper-smelting works, and an eighteen-mile band which ran from Blaenavon to Hirwaun, stretching along the northern rim of the coalfield. By 1815 this area contained eight large ironworks and an array of smaller ones. A large supply of the metal was needed for the production of munitions during the Seven Years' War of 1756–63 when supplies of the metal from abroad were curtailed. All the requisite raw materials were available in abundance in the area: iron ore, limestone for the flux used in smelting, coal for coking, and timber and stone suitable for building. London and Bristol merchants provided the necessary capital, and a number of ironmasters from the Midlands were the source of technical expertise.

John Guest from Broseley in Staffordshire came to manage the Dowlais works in 1759 (and started the Plymouth works in 1763), in which year also Anthony Bacon and William Brownrigg, Cumberland ironmasters, began the Cyfarthfa works, later bought by Richard Crawshay, a Yorkshireman. Bacon also purchased the Plymouth works from Guest, and made his fortune from cannon manufacture during the American War of Independence. In 1784, Francis Homfray and his son Samuel, like Guest natives of Broseley, set up works at Penydarren. Thus English ironmasters were responsible for the success of the four world-famous ironworks at Merthyr Tydfil. The iron boom was sustained by the need for military supplies during the French Wars of 1793–1815, by the arrival of the railway age at home and abroad in mid-century, and by the wide range of industrial and domestic products which made use of iron. By 1827 the south Wales iron industry was furnishing half of Britain's iron exports.

Technological change and experimentation were a vital ingredient in this success story, in particular the commercial availability of James Watt's improved steam engine in 1775, and the discovery in the 1780s of puddling, the 'Welsh method' of converting pig iron into malleable iron by decarbonizing it in a reverberatory furnace, perhaps first perfected by Henry Cort at his Hampshire ironworks. Homfray devised an iron floor for his furnaces in south Wales, and Wilkinson developed a new means of cylinder boring at Bersham. In 1838 an invention rendered possible the use of anthracite in blast furnaces, permitting the establishment of new ironworks in the western coalfield, particularly in the Amman and Gwendraeth valleys. But the introduction of the Bessemer process in 1856 (which greatly improved the quality of steel and reduced the time taken in its production) and of a new open-hearth process in 1867 rendered possible the use of steel for general construction use. These processes required imported ores and a relocation of the industry along the coast, at Newport, Cardiff, Port Talbot, Swansea and Llanelli.

## *The coal industry*

Coal, used in smelting, was initially no more than a branch of the iron industry. But south Wales coal began to be used in London as a domestic fuel in the 1830s and soon won favour abroad, particularly after the removal of the customs duty in 1834 and 1850. The railways and steam ships began to use more and more Welsh steam coal, increasingly favoured by many foreign navies and industries. These changes led to the opening up of new coalmines which were not associated with the iron industry, especially in the two Rhondda valleys where the seams lay far below the surface. Now the pioneers were native Welshmen, among them Walter Coffin and George Insole, both natives of Glamorgan. The construction of a rail network through the coalfield in the fifties and sixties heralded an enormous expansion of the industry when the unique richness of the deposits became fully appreciated. David Davies of Llandinam, taking a lease at Rhondda Fawr in 1864, became the foremost coalowner in south Wales and in 1887 formed the Ocean Coal Company Limited. It was he also who in the 1880s began to build a railway linking the Rhondda valleys with the new dock at Barry.

The upsurge of steam locomotives, steam ships and steam engines in industry seemed to guarantee prosperity. Many of the former iron companies became entirely coal-producing. In 1913, 57 million tons of coal were raised in south Wales, over half of it for export, and 250,000 miners were employed by the industry. Mining and export did not become important in the anthracite coalfield to the west of the Vale of Neath until after 1880 when anthracite was found to be admirably suited for use in closed stoves and central-heating systems. The countries fringing the Baltic and those in north-west Europe provided much-needed markets.

### *David Davies, Llandinam ('Top Sawyer')*

Born at Llandinam, Montgomeryshire, in 1818, he left school in 1829 to assist his father in the timber trade. In 1846 he was commissioned to build a bridge over the River Severn in his native village – a prelude to becoming a contractor for railway construction. He became the foremost coalowner in the Rhondda valleys, his coal-mines becoming incorporated into the Ocean Coal Company in 1887, and his construction of the dock at Barry in 1884 ensured the rapid development of that town. He amassed an enormous fortune, contributed generously to religious and educational causes, was a teetotaller and a devout Calvinistic Methodist. He served as the Liberal MP for Cardigan Boroughs from 1874 until 1886, was a governor of University College of Wales, Aberystwyth, from 1872 and represented Llandinam on the Montgomeryshire County Council from 1889. He died in 1890.

His grandson and namesake, who became the first Baron Davies of Llandinam, served as the Liberal MP for Montgomeryshire, 1906–29, founded the journal *The Welsh Outlook* in 1914, and displayed an abiding interest in peace and international affairs, helping to establish the Temple of Peace at Cardiff in 1938. Lord Davies's sisters, Gwendoline and Margaret, resided at Gregynog Hall near Newtown (now the residential conference centre of the University of Wales), were patrons of the Gregynog Press, and bequeathed their valuable art collection to the National Museum of Wales.

## Transport and communications

The new roads constructed in the wake of the Industrial Revolution linked the coalfields with the sea, the most important being Merthyr to Cardiff built in 1767, to which a branch road from Aberdare was added soon afterwards. Roads soon linked Merthyr with Swansea and Abergavenny. In each case the ironmasters were primarily responsible. The 'canal mania' which reached Wales during the last decade of the eighteenth century led to the expenditure of huge sums of money to overcome the problems posed by the hilly terrain. The Glamorganshire Canal, begun in 1791, joined Merthyr and Aberdare with Cardiff, while Newport was linked with Crumlin and with Abergavenny and Brecon. Canals also ran along the Neath and Swansea valleys, while Newtown and Welshpool were linked by canal to the River Mersey.

Although the canals provided cheaper transport than the roads, they were to be displaced from the 1850s onwards by tramroads and railways which often followed the same routes from the industrial centres to the coast. In February 1804 Richard Trevethick successfully ran his steam-driven locomotive, drawing a load of ten tons and seventy persons, from Penydarren to Abercynon – one of the first steam locomotives in the world. The Taff Vale Company opened a railway from Merthyr to Cardiff, the first major line in Wales, in 1841, surveyed by Isambard Kingdom Brunel, the great engineer. Other lines were soon built to connect Ruabon and Chester in the north, the industrial centres of Monmouthshire and Newport, and the Neath valley with Aberdare. In 1849 the Irish mails were for the first time taken by rail from Chester to Holyhead, a link of vital importance, and a line from Gloucester to Haverfordwest was completed in 1854. In 1864 Shrewsbury and Aberystwyth were finally connected by rail. The Severn Tunnel was completed in 1888.

## Telford's bridges

Thomas Telford (1757–1834) was a native of Dumfriesshire, Scotland, who became well known for his engineering work in Shropshire and on the Ellesmere Canal. He was responsible for the aqueducts over the River Ceiriog at Chirk (1796–1801) and over the Dee at Pontcysylltau (1795–1805), rightly hailed by contemporaries as 'among the boldest efforts of human invention in modern times'. Invited by the government of the day to turn his attention to the road from Shrewsbury to Holyhead, he designed a bridge over the Menai on the 'suspension' principle, then new to British engineers, to replace the hazardous Bangor ferry. Parliament having voted the necessary funds, work on the bridge extended from 1819 until 1825. Telford was also responsible for a similar bridge over the Conwy estuary, built in 1822–6, and for surveying the roads of south-west Wales. He is buried in Westminster Abbey.

One result of the building of a railway network was the rapid growth of towns and urban life in Wales. When the first census was taken in 1801, Merthyr Tydfil, with a population of 7,700, was by far the largest town in Wales. It retained its superiority in 1861 with a population of more than 50,000, but the subsequent decline of the iron industry meant that it was soon overtaken by other towns. The variety of industries in the neighbourhood of Swansea ensured a steady growth in population there throughout the nineteenth century, while Cardiff, a village with no more than 1,870 people in 1801, grew at an enormous rate after the opening up of the Rhondda valleys. The first dock had been built by the Marquis of Bute as early as 1839, but others were soon added, including Penarth in 1865 and Barry in 1889, both required to relieve the congestion at Cardiff.

## The effects of industrialization

Perhaps the most obvious visual result was the disfigurement of the countryside by furnaces, chimney stacks and rows of hideous houses. Many famed beauty spots were rapidly denuded of vegetation. In human terms the cost of industrialization was high. Towns sprang up, unplanned and uncontrolled, largely inhabited by uprooted and thus disorientated country folk who were often forced to live in congested conditions in jerry-built houses. The long terraces of workers' cottages had to be built one above another because of the narrowness of the Glamorgan valleys. Their water supplies were all too often polluted and their sanitary arrangements of necessity primitive; open sewers were common in many places. As a result outbreaks of typhus, typhoid fever and, from 1831 onwards, cholera were frequent, while respiratory illnesses were common. Infant mortality was especially high, and life expectancy low. Until the Mines Act of 1842 children often worked underground, while women were employed illegally in the mines until much later. Men worked excessive hours in dangerous and unhealthy conditions in coal-mines and metalworks alike, wages were generally low and often paid in tokens usable only in the company (or truck) shops where prices were unreasonably high for poor-quality food. Yet for many Welsh people such conditions were preferable to the hopeless poverty, inertia and lack of opportunities for advancement in the countryside. To many who migrated, the bustle, the sense of excitement and social cohesion of the industrial communities seemed adequate recompense and convinced them that they had improved their lot.

## Robert Owen

Born in 1771 at Newtown, Montgomeryshire, the son of a saddler-ironmonger. In 1781 he became apprenticed to a Scottish draper at Stamford, Lincolnshire. He became convinced that man's nature was influenced above all by his environment, a belief which he later claimed gave him 'illimitable charity' towards his fellows. He worked as a draper's assistant in London, and moved to Manchester in 1788 to seek his fortune. At the age of twenty he was appointed manager of a spinning mill with a work-force of about 500. In 1795 he became managing partner of the Chorlton Twist Company, and four years later bought the New Lanark works which were to make his name. Here he aimed to improve factory conditions, reduce working hours, educate factory children and introduce 'industrial harmony'.

His outstanding success at New Lanark as a pioneer of factory reform led him to advocate a state system of education and the provision of state-aided unemployment relief. He envisaged the establishment of 'villages of co-operation' where co-operative life would become an end in itself. From 1824 to 1828 he spent some £40,000 on a co-operative experiment at New Harmony, Indiana, USA, which ultimately failed. He became revered by many popular movements especially in America. His Grand National Consolidated Trade Union, formed in Britain in 1834, represented the culmination of Owen's attempts to organize labour, provided a peaceable outlet for the legitimate aspirations of the working classes and was a major fillip to the development of the trade union movement. During his last years he degenerated into self-righteousness and formed an Owenite 'religion' with its own hymns. He died at Newtown in 1858. In 1903 the Co-operative Union financed the building of the Robert Owen wing of the Newtown Public Library. A statue of him was erected in the town centre in 1956, and a museum to his memory opened in Newtown in 1983. His opinions have influenced the ideas of modern Welsh Socialism and of experiments in co-operative economy. One of his most important disciples in Wales was R.J. Derfel (1824–1905).

## Industrial discontent: the Merthyr Riots

Such conditions nurtured distress and discontent among the working classes, perpetually at the mercy of trade fluctuations. The harsh application of the poor laws was especially resented. The struggle for parliamentary reform encouraged the evolution of a self-awareness in these working classes, a new awareness of a seemingly inevitable antagonism between master and man, and Merthyr seems to have had a particularly active political tradition. The unprecedented rush of population in the 1820s, and uneven distribution of industry, coupled with a reduction in wages in 1831, exacerbated tensions. In June 1831 a crowd at Merthyr destroyed the building in which court records of their debts to tradesmen were kept. Some twenty people were killed in the exceptionally fierce riot which followed the dispatch of a troop of Highlanders to restore order. A detachment of the Swansea Yeomanry was disarmed by the rioters the following day. One of the leaders, Lewis Lewis, was transported for life, and Richard Lewis (Dic Penderyn), accused of wounding a Highlander, but protesting his innocence, was executed in Cardiff Gaol.

An Anti-Truck Act passed by the government in 1831 helped to curb the worst abuses of the system. Some workmen attempted to improve conditions by forming trade unions, but many iron-masters refused to employ union members. Bands of workmen known as the Scotch Cattle avenged themselves at night by attacks on 'non-union' men and employers in an attempt to impose solidarity in the 1820s, 1830s and even the 1840s. The emergence of the British trade union movement owes much to the efforts of a Welshman, Robert Owen, the son of a Newtown saddler.

## Chartism

Dissatisfaction with the limitations of the 1832 Reform Act and with the operation of the 1834 Poor Law Amendment Act were the motivating forces behind the growth of the Chartist movement which sought a charter of political reforms as the route to the salvation of the masses. Hugh Williams, a Carmarthen solicitor, sent emissaries to the country towns and the industrial districts of south Wales. In April 1839, a riot broke out at Llanidloes – a reaction to a depression in the flannel industry – which necessitated the calling in of troops. At Newport on 3–4 November a great demonstration proved a fiasco, for carefully laid plans were frustrated by a heavy storm which enabled the authorities to foil the efforts of the Chartists. Ten men were killed in front of the town's Westgate Hotel. The three leaders – John Frost, Zephaniah Williams and William Jones – were transported. Merthyr then became the centre of the movement in the forties and fifties, but by then it had lost much of its morale and support. Its leadership had proved irresolute and it was divided over methods and tactics. Yet it was an impressive working-class movement which bequeathed a legacy of political consciousness.

## *John Frost*

Born in 1784 at Newport. He was apprenticed to his grandfather father as a bootmaker and later worked as a draper's assistant in Bristol and London. He opened his own business in Newport in 1806 and married a local widow in 1812. In 1823 he was sentenced to six months' imprisonment, having been convicted of libel against Thomas Prothero, town clerk of Newport. He became active in local politics, was elected a town councillor in 1835 and held a number of civic positions, becoming Mayor of Newport. He was elected a delegate to the Chartist convention in October 1838. Frost was basically a moderating influence on Monmouthshire Chartism, but the feelings of local miners and ironworkers ran high. The march on Newport on 2 November 1839, in which Frost led the Blackwood contingent, proved a fiasco. Frost, in common with his fellow leaders Zephaniah Williams and William Jones, was originally condemned to be hanged and quartered for treason, but the sentence was changed to one of transportation for life. He was forced to undertake two years' hard labour because of a disparaging remark about Lord John Russell, the Colonial Secretary. He became indentured to a shopkeeper and worked as a schoolmaster. He was conditionally pardoned in 1854 and left for the USA, but returned home in 1856 to a hero's welcome and settled at Stapleton near Bristol where he died in 1877 in his ninety-third year.

# 8

# Politics, Nonconformity and Education

## Welsh politics

The nineteenth century witnessed the political awakening of Wales, brought about by persistent and profound social discontent. This awakening was in striking contrast to the political quiescence and inertia characteristic of eighteenth-century political life, and was occasioned above all by the staggering growth of Nonconformity. A small group of Nonconformists had lent support to the American and French Revolutions and had begun to campaign for an extension of the franchise and parliamentary reforms. An increase in their numbers coincided with the emergence of a substantial middle class of shopkeepers and tradesmen and of a large industrial proletariat. The Great Reform Act of 1832, although it did little to transform political life, had already raised the hopes and expectations of the unenfranchised masses; the resultant disappointment and disillusion led to support for the various movements for radical reform. The mood of popular discontent in the 1830s and 1840s was revealed in the activities of the Scotch Cattle, the Chartists and the Rebecca rioters. Direct action taken in the hope of attaining radical improvement of their social and economic conditions was the reaction of many of the Welsh, totally incapable as they were of influencing the processes of legislation and governed by men insensitive to their sufferings.

From about the middle of the century the real impetus of the demand for fundamental change came from the Nonconformist denominations who came to seek, above all else, the disestablishment of the Anglican Church and an extension of the franchise; other reforms, they felt, would inevitably follow upon the attainment of these objectives. From 1844 onwards the Liberation Society, which established many local cells in Wales, provided them with a coherent programme and an effective organization. Its work bore fruit with the 1867 Reform Act, which considerably widened the urban franchise, and with the Secret Ballot Act of 1872.

## *The periodical press*

One of the firmest indications of the growing social and political awareness in Wales was the emergence of a vigorous Welsh-language periodical press from 1814 to 1850. The publication of a new Welsh newspaper *Seren Gomer*, founded in Swansea in 1814, was one sign of a rebirth of interest in political discussion. Problems over distribution and the payment of tax meant that it survived as a weekly only until August 1815, but it reappeared as a monthly publication in 1818. Previously most of the columns in the Welsh press had discussed theological and cultural matters, but *Seren Gomer* began to consider the advocacy of free trade and the rights of the Welsh peasantry against their landowners, giving voice to the resentment against the payment of tithes. The even more radical *Efangylydd*, founded in 1830 by David Owen (Brutus), advocated the secret ballot and franchise reform. English-language newspapers also began to appear in Wales, among them the *Cambrian* (1804) in Swansea, the *North Wales Chronicle* (1807), and the *Welshman* and the *Carnarvon and Denbigh Herald* in 1832. These provided the Welsh middle class with a political education. Subsequently, 1835 saw the founding of the *Diwygiwr* and *Yr Haul*, while in 1843, the monthly *Y Cronicl*, edited by Samuel Roberts, and the fortnightly *Yr Amserau*, edited by William Rees (Gwilym Hiraethog), made their appearance. These papers readily advocated land reform, free trade and a system of elementary education. *Baner Cymru*, edited by Hiraethog under the influence of Thomas Gee, first saw the light of day in 1887, was amalgamated with *Yr Amserau* two years later, and soon attained a weekly circulation of 50,000 copies. Together with *Y Traethodydd* established by Dr Lewis Edwards of Bala in 1845, these publications exercised a profound influence on the development of Welsh thought and culture.

### Thomas Gee

Born in 1815 at Denbigh. In 1829 he became an apprentice at his father's printing works, he spent two years in London learning the trade and rejoined the family business in 1838. From 1845 he was responsible for the development of Gwasg Gee, a publishing press which produced a huge number of magazines, newspapers, books of poetry, academic and theological works. He became a confidant of many of the political and religious leaders of his day and was an influential figure in Welsh public life. He was a fervent Methodist, a regular preacher and a supporter of the Sunday Schools. Gwasg Gee was responsible for the production of the magazine *Y Traethodydd*, the encyclopaedia, *Y Gwyddoniadur Cymreig*, and the newspaper *Baner ac Amserau Cymru*, which was staunchly Liberal and Radical in outlook. Gee pressed for the provision of non-sectarian education for Nonconformists, the widening of the franchise, and the disestablishment of the Church, causes which he brought to the forefront of political life in rural Wales, although his influence on the industrial areas of south Wales was slight. He died in 1898. The business remained in the family until 1914 and continues to publish Welsh books and journals to this day.

## *The voice of Nonconformist protest and the Liberation Society*

The religious census of 1851 showed quite clearly that a large proportion of Welsh society, especially in the large towns, had no association with any place of worship. Yet it cannot be denied that Welsh Nonconformity had succeeded in capturing the interest of the Welsh working classes on a scale unknown elsewhere in Europe. The older Nonconformist denominations, the Baptists and the Independents, had inherited a corpus of radical ideas, both theological and political. Even the Methodists, while advocating political non-involvement, fully appreciated that their civic rights were inferior to those of practising Anglicans. As the evangelizing fervour of the Methodists affected the Baptists and the Independents, so too did the Methodists inherit the innate Radicalism of the older denominations, so that by mid century Welsh Nonconformists displayed a unity of protest against the privileges enjoyed by Churchmen.

From 1844 onwards the Liberation Society, although an English body, encouraged these Nonconformists to campaign for the abolition of the Established Church and for the removal of other disabilities, by introducing the idea of political strategy and organization into the Welsh constituencies. From the late 1850s the society adopted a more aggressive policy, enlisting the help of agents with extensive experience of political tactics and embarking upon propaganda tours of Wales in an effort 'to teach the people politics'. In this way a number of sects or groups in Wales were transformed into a 'Nonconformist nation'. Henceforth the needs of Nonconformity were to dictate the course of Radical politics.

## The election of 1859

This contest was held as a great religious revival swept over Wales, intensifying the feelings of Welsh Nonconformists and embittering their struggle against the Anglican landowners. In Merioneth, W.W.E. Wynne of Peniarth, the Conservative member, was especially disliked by Nonconformists because of his High Church principles. David Williams of Castell Deudraeth was persuaded to stand against Wynne, a move interpreted by local landowners as a threat to their privileged position. Tenants of the Rhiwlas estate near Bala who requested the right to abstain were personally interviewed by the landowner. Although Wynne was narrowly re-elected, three of the Rhiwlas tenants who had abstained and two who had ventured to vote for Williams were evicted from their farms. Evictions and harsh rent rises also took place on the Wynnstay estate, while in 1860 the tenants of a Cardiganshire landowner were ordered to become members of the Church of England or leave their lands. 'A thrill of horror' sped through Wales at these events for the exercise of economic pressure in elections had become evident to all. Subscriptions were raised to compensate the evicted farmers, while Merioneth electors sent petitions to Parliament advocating the secret ballot.

## The 1867 Reform Act and the election of 1868

The Reform Act of 1867 gave the vote to the industrial workers of the towns and to the tenants of small farms. As a result the Welsh electorate rose by about 263 per cent, that of Cardiff and Swansea increased more than three times and that of Merthyr a staggering ten times. Henceforth these industrial borough electorates contained a strong working-class element. At the same time a second parliamentary seat was awarded to Merthyr Tydfil. In the general election which followed in 1868, Merthyr Tydfil returned at the head of the poll Henry Richard, a notable pacifist and Nonconformist who represented the constituency until his death in 1888. He brought to the Commons the viewpoint of Welsh Nonconformity and underlined the necessity of organizing for peace in an age of triumphant nationalism and bloodshed throughout much of Europe.

Meanwhile, in 1868, Denbighshire returned to Parliament George Osborne Morgan, who, although an Anglican, was to become the foremost champion of Welsh disestablishment, powerfully supported by Thomas Gee. Twenty-one Liberal MPs from Wales sat in the 1868 Parliament, three of them Nonconformists. No fewer than seventy political evictions ensued in Cardiganshire and Carmarthenshire alone, powerfully denounced in the Commons by Richard and Morgan, who helped to secure the passage of the Secret Ballot Act in 1872, and who regularly brought Nonconformist grievances to the attention of their fellow Members. Further acts were passed in 1875 and 1883 which required landowners to compensate evicted farmers for any improvements which they had made to their holdings. The election of 1868 had inaugurated a new era (which was to last until 1922) when Liberal Radicals were to sit for the great majority of the Welsh seats.

### Henry Richard

Born in 1812 at Tregaron, Cardiganshire. He served as a Congregational minister in London from 1835 to 1850 and became Secretary of the Peace Society in 1848. He was known as 'the Apostle of Peace' in Wales, and became friendly with Richard Cobden. He travelled widely throughout Europe and encouraged the use of arbitration in international disputes. He was elected Liberal MP for Merthyr Tydfil in 1868, a victory which gave Welsh Nonconformity a voice in the Commons. He remained keenly interested in Welsh education, land reform, disestablishment, and the well-being of the Welsh language. He presented Welsh issues to a wider audience and became known as 'the Member for Wales'. He was a compelling and lucid writer in Welsh and English, particularly the latter as is clear from his *Letters on the Social and Political Condition of Wales* (1866), his many pamphlets and diaries. He was widely respected and did much to project the image of Welsh Nonconformist Radicalism. He died in 1888.

## Religious life: the influence of Nonconformity

The dramatic rise of Nonconformity influenced many aspects of Welsh life other than the political. Certainly, the chapels made enormous contributions to Welsh hymnology and literature. They also played an immensely important role in the growth of Welsh education through the Sunday School movement, the setting up of primary schools, and by supporting the movement for the establishment of a non-sectarian university in Wales. Their members were encouraged to practise the highest standards of public and private morality. Drunkenness was condemned with especial virulence; it was alarmingly prevalent in the first half of the century and a primary cause of social degradation. The passage of the 1881 Welsh Sunday Closing Act, which combined three of the concerns of Welsh Nonconformists – a sense of Welshness, teetotalism and respect for the Sabbath – was a clear indication of the influence of 'chapel power'. It was, moreover, the first piece of parliamentary legislation to grant Wales the status of a distinct national unit.

### Samuel Roberts

Born in 1800 at Llanbrynmair, Montgomeryshire, and educated locally, at Shrewsbury and at the Independent Academy at Llanfyllin. In 1827 he became co-pastor with his father of Yr Hen Gapel at Llanbrynmair. In 1843 he launched the journal *Y Cronicl* which was well received by Welsh Nonconformists. He opposed state intervention in education and protested virulently against the Blue Books report in 1847. He denounced slavery, English imperialism, the Crimean War and capital punishment, while supporting universal (including female) suffrage, temperance and railway building. He believed strongly that congregations should be free from centralized authority and was a consistent champion of the rights of the individual, fervently attacking landlordism (to which his own family had fallen victim). He also condemned the setting up of the Union of Welsh Independents in 1872, and the advent of industrial trade unionism. He emigrated to the USA in 1857 in an attempt to escape the hostility of the steward of the Wynnstay estate. The settlement proved a failure, and he returned to Wales within ten years where he remained until his death in 1885.

A large number of denominational newspapers and magazines were founded which helped to instil in their readership a social and political consciousness. The experience gained in ordering their internal affairs gave many Nonconformists a taste for debating and for the practical workings of democratic government, and some were later to play a part in local government following the passage of the 1888 Local Government Act when county councils assumed most of the administrative duties previously shouldered by the justices of the peace. Significantly, Thomas Gee became the first chairman of the Denbighshire County Council, a telling reflection of the decline in the influence of the squirearchy. Thus so many aspects of Welsh life were permeated by the impact of radical Nonconformity.

## *Disestablishment*

The rise of Nonconformity widened the gulf between the tenant farmers and their landlords and indeed between the industrial workers and the ironmasters, many of whom became associated with the gentry and readily adopted their Anglicanism. The third great Reform Act of 1884 gave the vote to farm labourers, and the redistribution of constituencies which followed in 1885 benefited Glamorgan and Monmouthshire. The tenant farmers, protected by the secret ballot, enjoyed a new freedom of action which resulted in the return of thirty Liberals for the Welsh constituencies in 1885 (and only four Conservatives), results paralleled by equally dramatic victories in the first county council elections four years later.

It was inevitable that Welsh Nonconformists would strive to secure the disestablishment of the Church of England in Wales. Many of the abuses of the eighteenth-century Church remained in the nineteenth. The bishops still failed to give spiritual leadership, many being non-resident, pluralist, political appointees with no Welsh associations. Even some of the lower clergy did not reside in their parishes; a few were members of the gentry, owning extensive lands themselves, or else served as land agents to landowning relatives. Many more were of far humbler origins, inadequately paid, illiterate, victims of drunkenness, all too ready to neglect their duties. Few had been able to afford a university education. Around the middle of the century a remarkable revival of efficiency took place in the Church, the creation of four outstandingly able reforming bishops, who reorganized their dioceses, reshaped the pattern of parishes and built new churches to cater for the spiritual needs of a rapidly growing and highly disorientated population.

Yet problems remained; most church or chapel-going Welsh people were Nonconformists, and the payment of tithes to an 'alien

Church' was highly resented, especially after the Irish Church was disestablished in 1869. Bills providing the same solution for Wales were regularly introduced in the Commons. In the 1880s the anti-tithe war broke out in north Wales, Denbighshire experiencing violent riots and the serious injury of several people. In 1891 a Bill was passed which made the tithe payable by the landowner, although in practice of course it was the tenant farmer who still paid. A number of disestablishment bills was introduced in the Commons during the 1892–5 Liberal Government, but none succeeded. Eventually, a bill became law in 1914, was suspended during the First World War, and was finally implemented in 1920. The Church was not only disestablished but disendowed and the money given to the University, the National Library and the county councils for national purposes. One victim of this change was the close association of Nonconformity and Liberal politics in Wales.

## Trade unionism

The eventual achievement of disestablishment was not the only event to influence the political life of Wales. Although trade unionism was not a significant force in Welsh life during the relatively prosperous 1850s and 1860s, the Amalgamated Association of Miners made much progress in 1869–71 and even achieved improved wages through successful strike action. But a further strike in 1875, bitterly fought by the coalowners, brought the union to bankruptcy and dissolution. The miners' defeat led to the setting up of the notorious 'sliding scale', championed by William Abraham (Mabon), whereby wage levels were tied to the selling price of coal. A further unsuccessful six months' strike in 1898 saw a new militancy and new leaders such as William Brace emerge in the industrial relations of the coalfield, and the South Wales Miners' Federation, well organized and highly militant, was formed. The sliding scale came to an end in 1902, and in 1908 an act was implemented which gave the industry an eight-hour working day. Four years later a Minimum Wage Act was introduced.

These reforms were deeply resented and hotly contested by the coalowners, now organized in powerful combines, and industrial relations rapidly deteriorated, as was shown by the 1910 Tonypandy riots. By the eve of the First World War, the south Wales coalfield was seething with industrial unrest against a background of regular pit accidents and widespread fatalities, most notably in 1913 at Senghennydd where an explosion underground killed 439 men and boys. In north Wales, too, the two great strikes of 1896–7 and 1900–3 in the slate quarries were the direct result of Lord Penrhyn's uncompromising opposition to the North Wales Quarrymen's Union, and there ensued a severe contraction in the Welsh slate industry.

### William Abraham ('Mabon')

He was born in 1842 at Cwmafan, Glamorgan, and educated locally. He became a tinplater, a miner and in 1870 a miners' agent. He played a part in the agreement which led to the drawing up of a sliding scale of wages in the coalfield in 1875 which related profits, prices and wages. From 1892 to 1898 the first Monday in each month became known as 'Mabon's Monday', when the miners had a day off in order to limit output and maintain wages. He was elected 'Lib-Lab' MP for the Rhondda in 1885, the first miners' representative from south Wales to become an MP, and sat for Rhondda West from 1918 to 1922. In 1906, the Labour party became a separate political organization to which the Miners' Federation became affiliated in 1909. Initially Mabon strove to preserve the autonomy of the small, independent trade unions in the south Wales coal industry, but failed in 1898 when the South Wales Miners' Federation was formed. He became President of the 'Fed' and attempted to exert a moderate, conciliating influence on the industry, but was eventually overtaken by more Radical miners' leaders such as Noah Ablett, Arthur Cook and Arthur Horner. He was also well known as a conductor of eisteddfodau and often sang to the audiences in a fine tenor voice. He helped to form *Cymdeithas yr Iaith Gymraeg* in 1885. He became a Privy Councillor in 1911 and died in 1922.

### *Welsh education*

There was no uniform or adequate network of schools in early nineteenth-century Wales. The Sunday Schools provided the major source of popular education; they were immensely influential, frequented by young and old alike, conducted in Welsh, and hugely popular. The schools of the National Society, an Anglican body founded in 1811, met with only a limited success as they inevitably incurred the opposition of Nonconformists, who formed their own body, the British and Foreign School Society, in 1814. The availability of government grants from 1833, treated suspiciously in Wales, did little to remedy the situation, so that there was only a handful of 'British Schools' in Wales by 1843, when Hugh Owen urged the Welsh to accept government assistance. In addition, there was a

*University College of Wales, Aberystwyth, Dyfed, founded in 1872 as a national university and partly dependent for the first ten years on collections made in chapels.*

number of 'private adventure schools', many (but not all) of which were inadequately staffed and badly housed, some thirty-four grammar schools, and a small group of remarkably competent private schools. The denominational academies, originally peripatetic, were becoming settled. These included the Presbyterian College, finally located at Carmarthen in 1795, and the Congregationalist Academies founded at Brecon in 1839 and Bala in 1842. An array of Methodist and Baptist academies followed, and in 1827 an Anglican college at Lampeter opened its doors, later to be the prestigious recipient of a university charter.

### Hugh Owen

Born in 1804 at Llangeinwen, Anglesey. He was educated locally and in 1825 he went to London to work as a clerk. In 1836 he became a clerk in the Poor Law Commission and was promoted to Chief Clerk in 1853. He had first come to prominence in 1843 when he published an open letter to the Welsh people on elementary education urging them to accept the schools of the British and Foreign Schools Society. He was active in the affairs of the National Eisteddfod, the Honourable Society of Cymmrodorion and the Normal College, Bangor, founded in 1858, which was the first college in Wales to admit Nonconformists. He was largely instrumental in the establishment of a college for the training of women teachers at Swansea in 1871 and the University College of Wales, Aberystwyth, in 1872. He resigned from the Poor Law Commission in order to devote himself to education, and pressed for an investigation into the state of intermediate education. His efforts culminated in the passage of the Welsh Intermediate Education Act of 1889 and the opening of the highly prized secondary schools throughout Wales. Yet he gave little consideration to uniquely Welsh problems and a low priority to the teaching of the Welsh language. He was knighted in 1881 and died in the same year.

## 'The Treason of the Blue Books'

The 1840s were a watershed in the history of education in Wales, witnessing far-reaching efforts on the part of the British and National Societies. In 1846 William Williams, MP for Coventry, secured the appointment of a commission to inquire into Welsh educational provision. This was conducted by three English barristers, assisted by eight colleagues, seven of whom were Anglicans. Their report was detailed and thorough, but they virulently attacked the standard of education provided, the competence of the teachers and the state of school buildings. Further, they claimed that wholesale ignorance and immorality prevailed throughout Wales and that these were the creation of the Welsh language, 'the language of slavery'. A storm of controversy and intense indignation arose in Wales; prominent Welshmen such as Henry Richard, Dr Lewis Edwards and Sir Thomas Phillips hastened to defend their native land. The incompetence of the commissioners and the unfair methods employed by them were pointed out. The comments of the commissioners made Nonconformists increasingly reluctant to accept State aid for education, and their relations with the Anglican Church became increasingly strained.

But eventually the report did stimulate increased activity; both the British and the National Societies opened new schools and new colleges. After the passage of Forster's Education Act in 1870, 'Board Schools' were set up in Wales as in England. Soon afterwards elementary education became both free and compulsory. The controversy engendered by the Blue Books report also had important political implications. It helped to shake the Methodists out of their political quiescence and thus created a united front of Radical and lively political dissent. Nonconformists were also made fully sensitive to their exclusion from the political system and power structure, and they launched renewed campaigns to achieve further electoral reform, a powerful fillip to the movements of Radical agitation in mid century.

## Secondary and higher education

The idea that Wales should have her own national university, raised by Owain Glyndŵr in the early fifteenth century and by Richard Baxter and others in the mid-seventeenth, was revived, principally by Hugh Owen, in the 1850s. Although initial approaches to Disraeli's government for financial aid in 1868 proved fruitless, plans to establish separate colleges in north and south Wales, funded by public subscription, were well advanced when the availability of a suitable building at Aberystwyth decided the choice of venue. This became the home of the University College of Wales which opened its doors in 1872. For the first ten years of its precarious and uncertain existence, it depended largely upon voluntary contributions made by the congregations of the Nonconformist chapels.

The recommendation of the Aberdare Committee in 1881 that there should be colleges in north and south Wales was implemented with the opening of colleges at Cardiff in 1883 and Bangor in 1884. All three colleges were soon to enjoy financial support from public funds, and were incorporated in a federal University of Wales in 1893. Colleges at Swansea, the College of Medicine in Cardiff and Lampeter were incorporated in the twentieth century.

A major problem facing the new colleges in the 1880s was the lack of adequately trained students from Welsh homes. The terms of the Welsh Intermediate Education Act of 1889 were revolutionary, for the new county councils were empowered to levy a half-penny rate for the provision of secondary education, the sum thus collected to be matched by a grant from central government on a pound for pound basis (a system later copied in England). Secondary schools opened their doors throughout Wales in the 1890s. In 1896 the Central Welsh Board was established to examine and inspect the schools. Wales therefore enjoyed much autonomy from England in her provision for secondary and higher education.

## Anglicization

Perhaps the major social effect of the Industrial Revolution upon Wales was the introduction of a substantial non-Welsh element into the population which could not be absorbed. Thousands of Englishmen, Irishmen and Scots remained distinct from the language and traditions of Wales. On the other hand, the industrial base of south Wales also provided a home for a significant number from rural Wales who would otherwise have been compelled to emigrate overseas. Anglicization grew rapidly after about 1870, and the values and popular culture of rural Wales were thus substantially displaced in the new valley communities. At the time of the 1871 census, no more than 34 per cent of the population of Wales was monoglot English-speaking. Thereafter large-scale migration from England combined with other factors to weaken the position of the Welsh language.

As has been seen, Welsh had little place in the various kinds of elementary education available, even before the arrival of the post-1870 Board Schools and the notorious 'Welsh Not'. In some communities monoglot English-speakers were revered and the English language seen as an obvious route to secure, well-paid, white-collar occupations. The Nonconformist ethic of improvement through self-help underlined the necessity of speaking English, which thus acquired an enhanced social function and was viewed as more important commercially and professionally. The Welsh language never became a significant political issue in the nineteenth century, while the young University College at Aberystwyth originally had no intention of teaching Welsh, and did so initially only through the medium of English, rather as a dead classical language might be taught. In political and educational circles the Welsh language was simply not viewed as an issue meriting attention. The concept of the 'bilingual man', whose Welsh was reserved for the hearth, the chapel and the eisteddfod alone, became deeply ingrained. Education, government and administration, business and commerce, were English territories.

Yet even in 1901 half the population of Wales could still speak the Welsh language, and 15 per cent were monoglot

Welsh-speakers. Indeed the *absolute* numbers of Welsh-speakers had risen steadily and had reached one million (compared with about 500,000 in 1800), but their position relative to total numbers was deteriorating sharply, and absolute numbers were soon to fall dramatically.

## Welsh national consciousness

Welsh national consciousness had been weakened over many centuries above all by the Anglicization of the gentry, the natural leaders of society and potential patrons of art and literature. Moreover, both the Anglican Church and the Nonconformist denominations formed an intrinsic, indivisible part of their English counterparts. The Industrial Revolution attracted a large non-Welsh population which could not be assimilated, and bound England and Wales more closely together economically. Welsh industry flourished as part of the general economic prosperity of Britain. Still closer links

*Ceremony of the* Gorsedd *of Bards at the annual National Eisteddfod.*

were forged by the building of roads and railways, most of which ran from east to west. As a result, Welsh culture came to be regarded as the culture of rural Wales. Wales had no unifying political organization and no central administrative bodies. Even the Courts of Great Sessions, the sole remaining autonomous instrument of government, were abolished in 1830 and replaced by two judicial circuits subject to the Westminster courts. Few Welsh voices were raised in protest at this final stage of a policy of union and assimilation initiated in 1536.

Yet some sense of Welsh national consciousness remained. The persistence of the Welsh language ensured at least a consciousness of difference from England. But there is no evidence of a conscious desire to preserve the language in the nineteenth century, let alone to establish institutions with that end in view. National sentiment was stimulated particularly by the antiquarian studies of the previous century and by the Romantic movement, especially influential in London-Welsh circles, and the Gwyneddigion Society still played an important role in encouraging the study of Welsh literature by publishing a quantity of Welsh poetry and prose from the Middle Ages. Between 1838 and 1849 Lady Charlotte Guest (wife of Sir John Josiah Guest, ironmaster of Dowlais) translated into graceful English the eleven tales of *The Mabinogion*. A popular edition of the complete work appeared in 1877. A new awareness of a great literary tradition thus grew up and became a powerful national force, and the Welsh language began to be viewed as the key symbol of Welsh nationality.

It was this Romantic revival which led to the rediscovery of the eisteddfod which has fostered literary production and encouraged the Welsh to literary and musical competition. The Cambrian Archaeological Association was founded in 1846 to study the antiquities of Wales. National consciousness was intensified still further in mid century by the mordant comments of the Blue Book commissioners and by the influence of nationalism on the Continent made familiar to Welsh audiences through the public lectures and writings of Gwilym Hiraethog and the activities of Michael D. Jones (leading to the founding of the Welsh colony at Patagonia) who depicted Wales, just like Italy and Hungary, as a 'nation rightly struggling to be free'. The idea that Wales was a separate nation was widely held by about 1860 after which it merged with a buoyant Welsh Radicalism to inaugurate a dramatic new era in Welsh political life. This era lasted until 1922, stimulated by the advance of democracy in 1867, 1872 and 1884–5, by the emergence of disestablishment as *the* Welsh question *par excellence*, by the impact of the great agricultural depression, and by the Irish example.

## Michael D. Jones

Born in 1822 at Llanuwchllyn, Merioneth, the son of the minister who became the first Principal of the Independent College at Bala in 1841. He was educated at Carmarthen Presbyterian College and at Highbury College, London. He went to America in 1847 and founded the Brython Association, which aimed to help Welsh immigrants. He developed the idea of establishing a politically independent second homeland for the Welsh people in north America. Later, realizing that the English language would inevitably be predominant in any community in the USA, he favoured locating the homeland in Patagonia. He later succeeded his father as Principal at Bala, but his tenure of the post was blighted by a long-standing quarrel over the government of the college.

He played an important part in the moves to establish the colony in Patagonia in 1865, contributed generously himself, and was obliged to sell his house to the college authorities, who subsequently sacked him. He was eventually allowed to remain on the staff of the college, but he resigned in 1892 to devote himself to the setting up of a new institution to be known as the Bala-Bangor Theological College. He wrote extensively in the Welsh press on social topics, was scathing in his attacks on landlordism and on 'the English cause', which encouraged Welsh-speakers to worship in English. He is justifiably regarded as 'the father of modern Welsh nationalism', who exercised a profound influence upon such figures as Tom Ellis, David Lloyd George and Owen M. Edwards. He died in 1898.

# 9

# Wales, 1880–1939

## *Political life*

The 1880s proved to be something of a turning-point in Welsh political life. The Reform Act of 1884 gave the vote to the tenant farmer and the farm labourer as well as to the miner and the steel and tinplate worker. The number of voters in the Welsh county seats increased from 74,936 to 200,373. The redistribution of constituencies which followed created 5 new county divisions (in place of 2) in Glamorgan and 3 (in place of 2) in Monmouthshire, and at the same time abolished 5 small borough seats. From 1885 to 1906 the great majority of Welsh seats returned Liberal MPs. In 1885, 30 of the 34 Welsh seats went Liberal, and of these 30 at least 14 returned Nonconformists. The new confidence and parliamentary strength of the Liberals led to spectacular progress in the campaigns to achieve land reform, education reforms, temperance legislation and Church disestablishment.

Although by the turn of the century, many local Liberal associations in Wales had become decadent and moribund, the party still made three net gains in Wales in the 'khaki' election of 1900, and in 1906 every seat in Wales returned a Liberal with the single exception of the second Merthyr seat which elected Keir Hardie of the Labour Representation Committee. Liberal Federations of North and of South Wales were created in 1886–7 and at Westminster a Welsh Parliamentary party came into existence. Among the new generation of Welsh Liberal politicians were Tom Ellis, Sam Evans, Ellis Griffith, William Jones, Herbert Lewis, D.A. Thomas and David Lloyd George, all of whom made a new, dynamic Welsh presence felt in British politics. This presence bore fruit in the Welsh Sunday Closing Act of 1881, the Welsh Intermediate Education Act of 1889, the appointment of a royal commission on Welsh land by Gladstone in 1892, and a succession of Welsh disestablishment bills.

At grass-roots level in the constituencies the party was sustained by shopkeepers and middle-class professional men in the local associations, by an array of local newspapers and periodicals, by its links with local government and with the buoyant staple industries of south and north-east Wales, coal, shipping and tinplate. The spirit of free trade, individual freedom and social equality, strongly backed by Welsh Nonconformity, had penetrated deep into the fabric of Welsh society.

### Tom Ellis

Born in 1859 at Cefnddwysarn, near Bala, Merioneth, the son of a tenant farmer. He enjoyed almost ten years' university education at UCW, Aberystwyth, and New College, Oxford, where he read History. He was elected Liberal MP for his native county in 1886 on a platform which strongly advocated Welsh home rule. He was a subtle and conscientious member at Westminster who did much to advance the causes of Welsh education, disestablishment and land reform. He was instrumental in securing the appointment of the Royal Commission on Land in Wales. He was idealistic, possessed a strong sense of Celtic identity and helped to found the *Cymru Fydd* movement in 1886. He became Junior Whip in 1892 and Chief Whip in 1894, thus sacrificing much of his early radicalism. He contracted typhoid in 1890 and thereafter suffered increasing ill health, exacerbated by overwork. He was a cultured, attractive personality, who never lost his close association with rural, Nonconformist Wales. He died prematurely in 1899.

## The impact of Labour

The victory of William Abraham (Mabon) as a Lib-Lab candidate in the Rhondda in 1885 did not undermine the Liberal hegemony in Wales. Nor did the Independent Labour party, formed in 1893, make very much impact upon the Principality. But the bitter strike of 1898 in the south Wales coalfield led to much heart-searching among younger miners' leaders that the conciliatory methods of Mabonism were outdated and brought about the establishment of the South Wales Miners' Federation. The Labour Representation Committee was formed in February 1900, and in the same year Keir Hardie won the second Merthyr seat as an LRC candidate. In 1901 the 'Fed' set up a fund to facilitate Labour candidatures in elections, and this bore fruit in 1906 when miners' representatives were returned for the Rhondda, Gower, South Glamorgan and West Monmouth, although Hardie remained the sole ILP Member. In spite of continued Liberal electoral success, Socialist ideas did make some progress in Wales through the ILP (there were twenty-seven branches in south Wales by 1905), the branches of the Plebs League and popular newspapers such as the *Merthyr Pioneer* and the *Clarion*. The Central Labour College, training school to a generation of Welsh Labour leaders, opened in 1909, while the quarrying areas of north Wales began to display an interest in Socialism, encouraged by the writings of Silyn Roberts and David Thomas in the Welsh language. The impact of Socialism was revealed in the nature of the industrial dissension of the immediate pre-war years. In October 1910 the Cambrian strike had begun in the Rhondda which culminated in the famous riots at Tonypandy in November. Two railway workers were killed by soldiers in the Llanelli riots of 1911. In the wake of such dissension the appeal of Syndicalist ideas grew, and the pamphlet *The Miners' Next Step* argued forcefully for the use of industrial means to withstand and undermine capitalist oppression.

## The economy and society

From about 1880 to the First World War, Wales was a land of striking contrasts. The rural areas of north and mid Wales initially at least remained sunk in depression, impoverished and insecure. The isolated pockets of industry which they contained – copper-mining in Anglesey, lead-mining in north Cardiganshire, woollen manufacturing in Montgomeryshire and Merioneth – were in steady, irreversible decay. The impact of the railways had cut into the coastal trade of small ports such as Portmadoc, Barmouth, Aberdyfi and New Quay. Most of the agricultural land was farmed by small-scale tenant farmers, few of whose holdings exceeded fifty acres. Only the great landowners owned estates exceeding 1,000 acres. Capital was lacking, agricultural techniques were primitive, and land hunger was acute. Economic problems were intensified by social divisions – a gulf between landlord and tenant in language, religion and political outlook, exacerbated all the more by the impact of the agricultural depression. The manifold grievances of the Liberal tenant farmers came to the surface in their evidence to the Royal Commission on Land in Wales, whose report appeared in 1896. Thereafter, however, agricultural conditions improved, prices rose, and some investment in new machinery occurred. The years 1901–11 actually saw an increase in the numbers employed on the land. The advent of county and parish councils, county schools and university colleges, a new confidence and breadth of outlook, helped to level out class distinctions and to build social bridges.

By contrast the years 1880–1914 in industrial Wales witnessed continuous, intense expansion of industrial production, manufacturing and commerce. Central to this buoyancy was the surging growth of the coal industry which dominated south Wales from the anthracite valleys of Carmarthenshire to the Rhymney and Sirhowy valleys of Monmouthshire, with outposts in the Wrexham-Rhos district of Flintshire and in southern Pembrokeshire. The coal production of south Wales rose from 16 million tons in the early 1870s to 30 million by 1891 and a staggering 56.8 million in 1913, one-fifth of the total British coal production. More than 250,000 men earned their living in the Welsh mines. The output was above all geared to the export market, and hence sensitive and vulnerable to foreign competition. Other industries survived on a much smaller scale alongside coal: iron and steel, the latter now firmly rooted on the coast; the tinplate industry, centred on west Glamorgan and east Carmarthenshire; the metallurgical industry in the hinterland of Swansea; and the slate-quarrying industry of Caernarfonshire and north Merioneth, which at its peak employed no fewer than 16,000 men.

Overall the frenzied expansion of industry brought about the growth of transport and other services, foremost among them perhaps the docks at Cardiff, Swansea, Barry and Newport, and the railway network for both passenger and freight traffic. The docks at Cardiff, especially the Bute Docks and the Roath Basin, were immensely active and prosperous, and Cardiff became the chief coal-exporting port in Britain, thus ensuring a vast fortune for the Marquis of Bute. An impressive display of Baroque buildings ringed Cathays Park in the centre of the city by the First World War, and Cardiff began to lay claim to the title 'capital of Wales' (a claim eventually recognized in 1955).

A distinctive, unique social world emerged in the coalfield valleys of the south, composed of the coalowners, their managers and overseers, a distinctive middle class of shopkeepers, professional men and an aristocracy of labour such as checkweighers and miners' agents, and a large, industrial, cosmopolitan proletariat growing in size at an amazing rate and acting as an irresistible magnet for rural Welsh, English and Irish people alike. Housing was generally substandard, overcrowding rife, health and hospital services primitive, poverty and ill-health common. Yet valley life possessed a richness and a vibrance, a thriving vitality, enriched by the multiplicity of Nonconformist chapels, friendly societies and institutes, singing festivals, theatrical and operatic societies, sporting activities, pubs and clubs. Communities were stable, relationships long-lasting, traditions appreciated, a fundamental identity of interest between the classes taken for granted. This cohesion was, as already noted, seriously undermined by the 1898 coal strike which bequeathed a new legacy of industrial conflict and class bitterness in such striking contrast to the conciliatory harmony of 'Mabonism', the old fabric of industrial peace.

## The national revival

The vague, unfocused sense of national identity which persisted to the third quarter of the nineteenth century formed the basis of a quite dramatic national renaissance from the 1880s. Writing and publishing in the Welsh language (already in decline) suddenly began to flourish again in a huge number of quarterly, monthly and weekly publications. A Society for the Utilization of the Welsh Language, seeking to extend the use of the language in the education system, was formed in 1885. This cultural vitality gave a new lease of life to the Nonconformist chapels, culminating in a famous revival in 1904, and a new status to the national eisteddfod, powerfully reorganized in 1880–1. Both chapels and eisteddfodau operated largely at a popular level. On a higher intellectual plane, the founding of the national university in 1893 helped to stimulate an impressive literary renaissance and the first serious attempts to chronicle the history of Wales, both of which were transmitted to the level of popular culture by Owen M. Edwards, founder of a remarkable range of Welsh periodicals. In this renaissance the spread of elementary schools, the opening of the highly cherished grammar schools, and founding of university colleges all played their part. The university was not the only symbol of national distinctiveness, for in 1907 royal charters were granted to a national library, to be located at Aberystwyth, and to a national museum, to make its home at Cardiff. In the same year a Welsh Department of the Board of Education was set up, with Owen M. Edwards appointed first Chief Inspector of schools.

### Owen M. Edwards

Born in 1858 at Coed-y-pry, near Llanuwchllyn, Merioneth. He was educated at the local Church school, Bala Theological College, UCW, Aberystwyth, Glasgow University and Balliol College, Oxford. He travelled extensively on the Continent from 1887 to 1889, and wrote equally extensively of his travels, before becoming Fellow and Tutor in History at Lincoln College, Oxford, in 1889. He remained in this post until his appointment in 1907 as Chief Inspector of Schools of the Welsh Board of Education, after which he exercised an enormous influence on the development of education in Wales.

At Oxford he helped to form *Cymdeithas Dafydd ap Gwilym*. From 1888 he published a large number of Welsh books and popular magazines and began a number of long-running series of volumes. He was the author of popular text-books on Welsh history. He launched his own monthly *Cymru* in 1891 and *Cymru'r Plant* in 1892, which by 1900 was selling 12,000 copies a month. The English-language *Wales* was a relative failure, as indeed were *Y Llenor* and *Heddyw*. He wrote books for children and in 1896 founded *Urdd y Delyn*, a forerunner of *Urdd Gobaith Cymru*. He made a major contribution towards achieving education in the Welsh language and made children aware of the traditions of their country. He wrote natural, readable Welsh which enabled generations of children to become familiar with the Welsh literary classics. He spent one year (1899–1900) as Liberal MP for Merioneth, but generally had little interest in politics. From 1907 he lived at Neuadd Wen, Llanuwchllyn, where he died in 1920.

The national revival also had its political aspect, many of the new generation of Welsh Liberal politicians becoming convinced of the need to create a movement to press for Welsh home rule on the Irish model. A *Cymru Fydd* League was formed in 1886 and survived for some ten years, but was the inevitable victim of persistent wrangling between north and south Wales, and never really succeeded in becoming a genuinely popular movement to achieve home rule. Tom Ellis died prematurely in 1899 and the ambitions of Lloyd George clearly lay at Westminster rather than within Wales. A home rule campaign headed by E.T. John in 1910–14 proved an embarrassing fiasco. The Welsh renaissance was, first and foremost, cultural, literary and educational, rather than separatist. The Welsh sought equality and recognition within the British system of government, not exclusion from it.

## The First World War

The majority of Welshmen, sympathizing deeply with the plight of the small, defenceless nations on the Continent, responded to the call to arms with a vigour and enthusiasm which were little short of miraculous. The readiness of Welshmen to join the armed services at least equalled that of the Scots and the English. Lloyd George's rise to become successively Minister of Munitions, Secretary for War and ultimately Prime Minister was viewed euphorically throughout Wales. Patriotic fervour and war hysteria seemed compatible companions. The by-election which took place in Merthyr following the death of Keir Hardie in 1915 clearly showed that war enthusiasm transcended international Socialism even in the Socialist stronghold of Wales.

There were, of course, elements opposed to the war – the membership of the Union of Democratic Control, members of the Welsh intelligentsia who founded the journals *Y Wawr* at the University College of Wales, Aberystwyth, in 1915 and *Y Deyrnas* in 1916. Conscientious objectors were generally harshly treated. The introduction of military conscription in 1916 inevitably led to much soul-searching among Welsh Liberals, and the whole-hearted support for the war, so apparent in 1914, had clearly waned by 1917. The massive loss of life in the trenches, combined with the attacks on civil liberties, caused profound disillusion. Few Socialists had remained true to their pacifist traditions at the outbreak of the war. Only a handful of Independent Labour party stalwarts who opposed the war suffered imprisonment. Indeed many workers relished the prospect of higher wages provided by the war. Many Welshmen achieved important posts in central government by hanging on to Lloyd George's coat-tails.

The impact of the war upon Wales was considerable. The State intervened in people's lives on a scale hitherto unknown. Industries and agriculture were controlled by government boards, the mines and the railways put under public control, social provision vastly expanded. Subsidized houses were built on a large scale, the Fisher Act of 1918 radically reformed public education, health and hospital provision was improved, many commodities including food were rationed, and prices were subjected to controls. Generally wages rose and living standards improved in rural and industrial areas alike. Trade union membership, rights and status increased dramatically, and economic prosperity and success continued. The demand for Welsh coal appeared unlimited and insatiable, as indeed did the demand for Welsh milk, livestock and corn. Tenant farmer and farm labourer prospered, both savouring the effects of the Corn Production Act of 1917, but the problems of the landowner, the victim of falling rents at a time of severe inflation in land values, multiplied. Thus large portions of many major estates were sold, in many cases to their tenants, during what became a 'green revolution'.

## David Lloyd George

Born in 1863 in Manchester and brought up at Llanystumdwy, Caernarfonshire, by his widowed mother and his revered Uncle Lloyd. He became a solicitor at Cricieth in 1885, and was elected Liberal MP for Caernarfon Boroughs in a by-election in 1890. He was initially at Westminster a spokesman for Nonconformist grievances and the rising Welsh nationalism of the 1890s, but he soon became more identified with general British Radical issues. He became President of the Board of Trade in 1905 and Chancellor of the Exchequer in 1908, when he furthered schemes of social welfare including old-age pensions and national health insurance. The rejection by the House of Lords of his People's Budget of 1909 (which greatly increased taxation to finance social reform) ultimately led to the Parliament Act of 1911. During the First World War, he became Minister of Munitions in 1915, Minister of War in July 1916 and Prime Minister in December 1916. But he split the Liberal party irretrievably, a split intensified in the 'Coupon' Election of 1918 when he was overwhelmingly re-elected at the head of a Conservative-dominated coalition. The coalition collapsed in 1922, Lloyd George fell from power, and was never to hold office again.

He was elected leader of a reunited Liberal party in 1926, and made a superhuman effort to return to power in 1929, but in vain. His last effort was his Council of Action for Peace and Reconstruction in 1935. He intervened in the Commons in May 1940 in a powerful speech in which he demanded

Chamberlain's resignation. He still retained much support in rural Wales, and remained a familiar figure at the National Eisteddfod, delighting audiences with his oratory and wit. In January 1945 he was elevated to the peerage as Earl Lloyd-George of Dwyfor, but died in March. He lies buried near the River Dwyfor at Llanystumdwy. In a sense he gave Wales a new political status as a nation and a new-found political reality.

In the south the temper of industrial relations was transformed by the growth of tension and industrial bitterness, a new social militancy and the spread of advanced 'Socialist' ideas reflected in the radicalization of the all-embracing 'Fed'. The Welsh miners were virulently opposed to the introduction of military conscription, deeply resented the massive profits made by some businessmen, and warmly greeted the Bolshevik Revolution in 1917. The government responded by appointing a Commission of Industrial Unrest which painted an alarming picture of deteriorating conditions. Belligerence increased in 1918, fuelled by high rents and food shortages, and the young Labour party reaped the benefit – reflected in the founding of constituency parties and the appointment of full-time agents.

The impact of war had indeed been profound. At the very least it had acted as a catalyst or stimulant, accelerating processes of political transformation, economic dislocation and social and cultural change already perhaps at work before 1914. The Wales which emerged five years later had changed almost beyond recognition, but the nature of these changes had been apparent long before 1914.

## Post-war Wales

For a short time the patriotic frenzy of 1914 persisted and is reflected best in the outcome of the 'coupon' election of 1918 when supporters of Lloyd George's Conservative-dominated Coalition were re-elected in 25 of the 36 redistributed Welsh constituencies. Even so Labour captured 10 industrial seats and 30 per cent of the popular vote in

Wales, and became the official opposition at Westminster. But the mood of wartime patriotism soon evaporated, giving way to intense disillusion and despair, and to the birth of a new kind of Welsh society. In June 1920 the Welsh Church was finally disestablished in the midst of mass apathy and indifference. The dominance of the landed gentry disappeared too, as the sale of the great estates continued unabated, reaching its climax in 1918–22. The Liberal hegemony was visibly crumbling, bitterly divided into Lloyd Georgite and Asquithian factions as was reflected in a savage by-election in Cardiganshire in 1921. In the industrial south a series of by-elections provided an array of Labour gains, successes consolidated in the general election of November 1922 when the Liberals retreated to assume the role of, at best, the party of rural Wales. This general pattern of growing Labour dominance was confirmed in 1923 and 1924, by which time Welsh Liberalism in particular had become more and more decadent and stagnant, totally remote from the problems of the miner and the steelworker. Traditional Liberal issues – disestablishment, local home rule, temperance legislation – appeared totally irrelevant to the post-war generation, and Labour began to reap the benefit of active Nonconformist support, formerly the preserve of the Liberals.

By the early twenties the Labour movement in south Wales had become much more aggressive and class-conscious. Extreme syndicalism flourished in the Rhondda. The leadership of the miners' union had passed into especially militant hands such as those of A.J. Cook, Arthur Horner and Frank Hodges. In 1919 Lloyd George and Bonar Law failed to implement the majority recommendation of the Sankey Coal Commission that the mines should be nationalized, a decision which brought enormous dismay and bitterness in south Wales, felt even more keenly with the huge loss of trade and mounting mass unemployment which befell the industry at the end of 1920. A national miners' strike took place from March to July 1921 after which the miners were compelled to return to work on the owners' humiliating terms. The much proclaimed Triple Alliance of miners, railwaymen and transport workers broke down ignominiously, further adding insult to injury. Predictably, some of the new generation of militant young miners gravitated towards the Communist party formed in 1920 in Britain. But the Communists did not reap the same kind of success in parliamentary elections in Wales as in Scotland and east London. The influence of the Central Labour College was especially in evidence, its products including Ness Edwards, Jim Griffiths, Morgan Phillips and Aneurin Bevan, all of whom remained within the mainstream trade union and Labour movement.

The Nonconformist chapels began a steady and irreversible decline in support and influence, especially among the industrial and urban masses of the south, a decline accelerated by the fall in the numbers speaking the Welsh language. Working men in particular were more impressed by the secular appeal of Socialism and trade-union activity, by the miners' lodges and the Workers' Educational Association classes, by the pubs and the clubs. The advent of the motor car and the radio challenged still further the traditional Welsh Sunday. There was, moreover, a marked change in attitudes towards Welshness and nationalism. The ideas of *Cymru Fydd* seemed dated and irrelevant in post-war Wales. Some people turned to embrace a wider concept of internationalism and support for the League of Nations. A Welsh branch of the League of Nations was formed in 1922. Others embraced a new and heightened nationalism, disillusioned by the abysmal failure of a number of national conferences convened between 1918 and 1922, and by the empty protestations of Liberal and Labour parties alike. The efforts of E.T. John were from the outset doomed to futility. Time and time again the claims of Wales were disregarded when administrative devolution took place. The result was the formation in August 1925 of *Plaid Genedlaethol Cymru*, a fiercely autonomous, nationalist political party, which sought, first and foremost, to defend the Welsh language, and which soon won over many of the Welsh intelligentsia, but gained little popular support. One of its founders and its major theoretician, Saunders Lewis, became the party's president in 1926. For Plaid Cymru, a long, slow road lay ahead. Its formation was, in many ways, one of the effects of the war upon Wales.

### Saunders Lewis

He was born in 1893 at Wallasey, Cheshire, to a notable Calvinistic Methodist family. He was educated at the Liscard High School for Boys and at Liverpool University. He served with the South Wales Borderers during the First World War, returned to university and graduated in English. He wrote a thesis on eighteenth-century Welsh poetry which was subsequently published as *A School of Welsh Augustans* (1924). He became a librarian in Glamorgan in 1921 and a lecturer in Welsh at University College, Swansea, in 1922. He was one of the founders of *Plaid Genedlaethol Cymru* in 1925, became its president in 1926, and was received into the Roman Catholic Church in 1932. In 1936, together with D.J. Williams and Lewis Valentine, he set fire to building materials assembled at Penyberth, Caernarfonshire, for the construction of an RAF bombing school. He was imprisoned, dismissed from his post, and subsequently earned his living from journalism, farming and occasional teaching, until he was appointed lecturer in Welsh at University College, Cardiff, in 1952, where he remained until his retirement in 1957. Thereafter at his home at Penarth he withdrew from active politics and devoted himself to his writing. His BBC Wales Radio Lecture for 1962 *Tynged yr Iaith* brought about the formation of *Cymdeithas yr Iaith Gymraeg*. He was a prolific political journalist, a literary critic and an outstanding creative writer who excelled in all the literary genres: poetry, plays and novels. His literary criticism did much to illuminate the work of the great *cywyddwyr* of the fourteenth and fifteenth centuries. He is generally considered to be the greatest literary figure in the Welsh language of the twentieth century. He died in 1985.

## The Depression

The prosperity of the immediate post-war years soon came to an abrupt end. As early as the autumn of 1920 the coal, steel-making and shipbuilding industries suffered the beginning of a severe slump which was to last fifteen years. Such a high proportion of Welsh working men was employed in the extractive industries that Wales was especially ill-equipped to withstand the profound stagnation of trade and industry, and could benefit but slightly from the demand for consumer durables and motor cars which grew up in the thirties. Welsh unemployment rose from 13.4 per cent in December 1925 to 23.3 per cent in December 1927 and to 27.2 per cent in July 1930, at which time the proportions for England and Scotland were 15.8 and 17.9 respectively. In the coal-mining valleys the Depression was at its most severe; Cardiff, Swansea and parts of north Wales benefited from a more diverse occupational structure.

The major reasons for this depression were the enormous loss of overseas markets and the declining use of coal in the world's mercantile marine. No recovery came until after 1936 with the impact of rearmament and improved international trading. The Welsh steel and tinplate industries were equally ill-equipped to face the challenge of depression, while Welsh agriculture, too, had its own difficulties: the level of mechanization was low, the quality of beef and lamb was generally poor, and the marketing of products badly organized. Successive governments did little to tackle the crisis until after 1933; the radical ideas of the economist J.M. Keynes were rejected out of hand by all except Lloyd George who was simply not trusted. Relief was provided in the main by the voluntary efforts of the Quakers and other groups. Government action did not come until 1934 with the passage of a Special Areas Act and subsequent efforts to attract new industries. The Treforest trading estate near Pontypridd received its first factory in 1938. Overall, government efforts were feeble in the extreme.

The results of all this were calamitous: shops and entertainments declined, community life, especially that of the chapels, shrank, there was large-scale migration to the south-east of England and to the Midlands. Some 430,000 left Wales between 1921 and 1940. Dire poverty and hardship were rife, local authority finances collapsed, working-class housing decayed still further, the state of public health was alarming. The report of an inquiry into the anti-tuberculosis services in Wales which appeared in 1939 painted a grim picture of housing and public health in much of Wales. Yet life went on even in the south-east coalfield valleys, which suffered more than the anthracite coalfield to the west and the coastal ports to the south. Life became intensely local, revolving around the miners' clubs and libraries, welfare halls and institutes, cinemas and billiard rooms, and local 'Co-ops'. A cohesion and a self-reliance emerged in these communities, a sense of isolation and detachment which survived to the 1960s and beyond.

## The Labour ascendancy

The inter-war depression coincided with the consolidation of a period of Labour ascendancy in the political and social life of Wales. As early as 1922 Labour polled 40.8 per cent of the total vote in Wales. Its rise seemed to be consolidated by the mass unemployment, intense hardship and industrial conflict of the 1920s. The south Wales valleys became the stronghold *par excellence* of the Labour party in Britain, an ascendancy extended to the county councils of Glamorgan and Monmouth and to the urban district councils within them. Most of the new generation of Welsh Labour MPs were prominent trade union officials, former miners and miners' agents. Few were destined to become high-flyers at Westminster. The main challenge to Labour in the late 1920s came from Lloyd George's revitalized Liberal party with its dramatic and advanced new programmes to tackle the scourge of unemployment. Although the Liberals polled 33.5 per cent of the votes in Wales in the election of 1929, they won only 10 seats, and seemed condemned to represent at best rural Wales. Labour won 25 Welsh seats including Carmarthen and Brecon and Radnor as well as its industrial strongholds. Even in 1931, when Labour secured no more than 46 seats throughout Britain, it returned 16 Members from industrial south Wales in a block extending from Llanelli to Pontypool. Lloyd George by the 1930s was becoming increasingly remote from Welsh life, and indeed from the mainstream of British politics. The Welsh Labour party in the Commons included Aneurin Bevan from 1929, S.O. Davies from 1934 and James Griffiths from 1936.

The growing march of political Labour was paralleled by the industrial conflict which culminated in the general strike of May 1926, a nine-day wonder, and a six-month stoppage in the coal industry. South Wales displayed a remarkable solidarity, and the failure of the strike bequeathed a huge legacy of bitterness, bewilderment and despair, intensified still further by the ruthless victimization which followed the return to work. The resources and membership of the South Wales Miners' Federation inevitably declined, soon to be challenged still further by the growth of company unionism and large numbers of blacklegs. The impact of the so-called Spencer Unions increased class bitterness still further. The political ascendancy of Labour remained unchallenged, even by the Communists, and penetrated deep into the heart of the industrial communities, its local representatives remaining an intrinsic part of the communities from which they had sprung. The public services of local Labour councillors and aldermen were immensely valuable; they did their utmost to remove slum housing and improve the standard of health care and welfare services, and they fought unflinchingly against the harshest enactments of the National Government. These local representatives helped to create a network of social activity and resourcefulness which held communities together in the face of adversity and hopelessness.

# 10

# Modern Welsh Society

## *The Second World War*

The civilian population was far more involved in the Second World War than it had been in the Great War of 1914–18. Collectivist tendencies increased, the employment of women became widespread, working-class living standards rose, and class differentials were eroded. Yet the war of 1939–45 was not such a traumatic turning-point in the history of Wales as the holocaust of 1914–18. There was much greater unanimity of support for the war in 1939 than in 1914. It was widely held that this was a people's, indeed a workers', war. The Labour party had voiced its opposition to Fascism from the outset. From 1939 to 1941 the Communists condemned the war as an imperialist crusade against Germany, and the party's Welsh membership fell substantially from its peak in 1938. It recovered somewhat after 1941; in the general election of 1945 Harry Pollitt won 45 per cent of the poll in Rhondda East and was defeated by only 972 votes. Plaid Cymru declared its neutrality at the outbreak of war. However, most of its supporters ultimately played some role in the war, with only a small number resisting conscription on nationalist grounds.

Widespread fears were expressed in 1939 that the Welsh identity would be destroyed by the War Office's possession of large tracts of rural Wales and by the influx of evacuees from English cities. The government's intention of moving four million mothers and children from England was never fulfilled, but large numbers did migrate, many on their own initiative, especially from London and Merseyside. They were absorbed effortlessly in much of Welsh

Wales. Elsewhere steps were taken to counter the linguistic threat; a Welsh elementary school was opened at Aberystwyth, and a defence committee was formed to care for the welfare of Wales, a committee which became known as *Undeb Cymru Fydd* in 1941.

Although it was felt initially that Wales would not be a target for the German Air Force, Cardiff, the south Wales valleys and above all Swansea endured a number of devastating attacks. There were forty-four attacks on Swansea from 1940 to 1943, the worst in February 1941 when 230 people were killed and the town centre was destroyed. In all 985 civilians were killed in south Wales during 1941 alone.

The social effects of the war were considerable. Twenty-two per cent of employed workers were in the armed forces by 1944, and a further 33 per cent were engaged in civilian work associated with the war. Unemployment had all but disappeared. Some 100,000 left Wales for England, many of them women compelled to migrate by the government. Within Wales many women found employment, particularly in the arms factories such as that at Bridgend. The attempt to diversify the structure of the Welsh economy had already begun; by 1945 20 per cent of the Welsh work-force were factory workers compared with only 10 per cent in 1939, while the proportion of men employed in the extractive industries had fallen from 30 to 20 per cent. So severe was the shortage of miners by 1944 that the Bevin Boy scheme was devised to conscript young men for the coal-mines. Some 100,000 miners went on strike in Wales in 1944 to protest against the policy of 'thinning out' the labour force in their industry. Living standards certainly rose as a result of the war. Although inflation rose by 42 per cent from 1939 to 1943, the wages of the working class in Wales at least doubled during the same period.

## Restructuring the economy

Unemployment fell sharply in Wales in the early 1940s, more as a result of the war than of any regional policy of the government. The cessation in the output of munitions and weapons in 1945 released manufacturing floorspace for light industry and bequeathed an industrial work-force, male and female, skilled in factory operation. The determination of Attlee's Labour Government, elected in 1945, that the unemployment levels of the interwar years should never be repeated, coupled with a universal acceptance of Keynesian economics, resulted in the passage of the Distribution of Industry Act, 1945. This measure sanctioned the utilization of existing factory space in Wales, and added to it by the provision of advance factories, the creation of new industrial estates at Bridgend, Hirwaun and Fforestfach, and the awarding of grants and low-interest loans to incoming industries. Two development areas were designated in Wales: one in the south, comprising the entire coalfield, the Vale of Glamorgan and Gower, and another in the north-east industrial belt. Industrial growth was to be restricted in the most successful areas.

The Attlee Governments of 1945–51 nationalized the Bank of England, the coal and steel industries, the railways, the docks, electricity, gas and road transport. Each was to be run by a central board. In a Welsh context, the most important of the nationalized industries was coal. Although the numbers employed by the industry had fallen from 270,000 in 1921 to 115,000 in 1947, this was still the largest single body of Welsh workers, and Nationalization day, 1 January 1947, saw widespread rejoicing throughout the coalfield valleys. By 1950 the proportion of Welsh workers in the employ of the government, directly and indirectly, had risen to more than 40 per cent, double the national average, reflecting the predominance of the nationalized industries in the Welsh economy and the increasing numbers employed by the public services, especially education, and local and central government. The national identity of Wales was, however, largely ignored; the organization of the gas industry alone regarded Wales as a national entity with the creation of the Wales Gas Board.

The policies of the Labour governments of 1945–51 were to some extent maintained by the Conservative administrations of 1951–64, and met with considerable success. The development areas welcomed a flood of new industries: components of the vehicle industry, electrical goods, mechanical engineering, timber and furniture, chemicals, clothing, paper and printing, and textiles. Particular success was achieved in attracting new firms in 1945–51 and in 1964–75. By the mid-sixties general manufacturing accounted for 30 per cent of the Welsh work-force, compared with 11 per cent in 1939, and employment opportunities in offices and in the public services had increased substantially.

Economic expansion was also facilitated by investment in new roads and motorways and in the building of new towns such as Cwmbran in Gwent and Newtown in Powys, as well as by the newfound prosperity of the nationalized steel industry. The alternation of governments at Westminster brought fluctuating industrial fortunes. The steel and coal industries contracted in the mid-fifties following a period of economic freewheeling. Much of north-west Wales was made a development area by new legislation in 1958, and further enactments followed in the sixties. The market towns of mid and west Wales welcomed small-scale light manufacturing industries introduced through government support which provided employment for many former farm labourers displaced by increasing mechanization. Yet problems remained. For much of the period after 1945 Welsh unemployment remained at double the national average, while female employment lagged behind England, as indeed did the capital assets and annual expenditure of the individual. The Wilson Government elected in 1964 attempted to remedy the situation; the Royal Mint was moved to south Wales and the Welsh Development Agency was created. Many of the intrinsic weaknesses of the Welsh economy were dramatically highlighted in the 1980s with the contraction of the coal and steel industries, the economic difficulties of the whole of western Europe, and a sharp decrease in public spending. Inevitably many of the multinational and English companies which set up factories in Wales concentrated production in their home factories in time of recession, while access to English and European markets has frequently been a problem.

## Rural Wales

Rural depopulation became a major feature of Welsh life after 1945. For those who remained to farm, a new-found prosperity resulted from the 1947 Agriculture Act, with increased production, steadier price levels and expanding markets. Some eighty per cent of Welsh farmers participated in co-operative schemes for storing, grading and marketing produce, and many increased the size of their holdings by absorbing the land of their neighbours. Even so, most Welsh farms continued to be relatively precarious, small-scale enterprises. The formation of the Farmers' Union of Wales in 1955 was one reflection of a sense of insecurity and vulnerability. Inevitably, the post-war period saw a fall in demand for agricultural labourers and rural craftsmen such as blacksmiths and saddlers. At the same time the small-scale industries of rural Wales were declining. The slate-quarrying industry of Gwynedd contracted severely after 1945 so that by the early seventies only five quarries employing a tiny handful of men remained in operation. Some recovery took place subsequently, stimulated by a buoyant tourist demand for slate ornaments and clocks. The woollen industry and clothing manufacture were also visibly in decline. This pattern was relieved by a few new initiatives – the opening up of the Rio Tinto Zinc Corporation's aluminium reduction plant near Holyhead in 1970, the establishment of power stations at Trawsfynydd in Merioneth and Wylfa Head in Anglesey, and the activities of the Forestry Commission in much of rural Wales. Yet overall the story was primarily one of decay, relieved only by thriving tourism during the summer months and the influx of elderly residents seeking a peaceful retirement. This trend was intensified by the closure of a number of key railway lines in the mid-sixties following the recommendations of the infamous Beeching Report in March 1963. Difficulties were compounded in the eighties and nineties because of ever-accelerating rural depopulation, the unrelenting influx of immigrants from England, the introduction of harsh quotas on milk production from 1984, and substantial cuts in agricultural subsidies which resulted in a cumulative loss of 24,000 jobs in the Welsh farming industry by 1998. Also, by the end of the nineties, agricultural farm incomes had attained a record post-war low, while successive governments – Conservative and Labour alike – seemed half-hearted in their response to repeated pleas for assistance, and substantial numbers of Welsh farmers faced bankruptcy and ruin.

## Changing patterns of employment in the 1980s and 1990s

By May 1979, when the Conservatives took office, 43 per cent of the Welsh working population were employed in the public sector. The new government's determination to reduce public expenditure inevitably had a disproportionate impact upon Wales. During the next four years, employment in the steel industry fell by 70 per cent, in manufacturing by 17 per cent and in construction by 21 per cent. There was no compensatory growth in the service sector so that Welsh unemployment, which ran at 8.5 per cent in 1979, had risen to 16.7 per cent by May 1983. Not a single coal-mine remained in the Rhondda valleys by the mid-1980s. Output fell from 28 million tons in 1947 to 18 million in 1968 and 11 million in 1978, by which time no more than 36,000 men were employed by the industry. By the end of the 1980s a mere five 'deep' pits in south Wales and one in the north remained operational, providing employment for a work-force of no more than 4,000.

During the miners' strike of 1984–5 the miners of south Wales displayed a remarkable solidarity and dignity at a time when the profound sense of communal identity in the south Wales valleys had inevitably come to an end. The new industries which had succeeded coal often required lengthy commuting, employed a high proportion of women and had different patterns of trade union membership. The Welsh industrial economy underwent decline and subsequent regeneration in 1983–7, and a new optimism had begun to emerge by the time Mrs Thatcher went to the country in June 1987.

Nevertheless, Wales faced formidable economic problems throughout the 1990s, and these were exacerbated by an uneven distribution of foreign investment, substantial redundancies in the steel, tinplate and coal industries, and a sharp increase in the collapse of small industries such as the Brymbo steelworks near Wrexham and the severe contraction of once prosperous concerns like the Laura Ashley Company. Large cuts in agricultural subsidies led to the loss of thousands of jobs in the farming industry.

Some 9.4 per cent of the Welsh populace was unemployed by the end of 1991. About 2,000 businesses had collapsed by the end of the same year, while the closure of the Penallta colliery in Ystrad Mynach had by 1992 reduced the number of working miners in south Wales to fewer than 1,000 employed in only three collieries, a trend intensified still further by the decision to close the Tower colliery in the Cynon Valley. The effects of the recession persisted above all in the industrial valleys of the south and in the north-east, and were intensified by a sharp fall in government grants from £197 million in 1981 to £134 million a decade later. David Hunt's high profile 'Rural Initiative' proved of little avail, Welsh rates of pay and income per head lagged far behind much of the United Kingdom, and the incidence of homelessness increased. Agricultural incomes fell to their lowest levels since 1945, calls for increased governmental support for rural communities fell on deaf ears, and by the mid-1990s it was widely believed that Wales was not receiving its due share of assistance from the EC. The Welsh housing market was generally feeble and, although government statistics indicated that Welsh unemployment had fallen from 10 per cent in 1993 to 7.5 per cent by the end of 1996, there was widespread concern that the true level was much higher, with unemployment amongst the male and youth population being particular causes of concern.

### The rule of Labour

The Second World War confirmed the move to the left initiated during the twenties and thirties. In the general election of 1945, Labour secured 58.5 per cent of the popular vote in Wales (recording a swing of 12 per cent) and won 25 seats, 21 of them with an absolute majority. With the single exception of the East End of London, Wales had become the least Conservative region of the United Kingdom. The same election was a severe blow to the Liberals who won only 12 seats nationally, 7 of which were in rural Wales. Indeed the only seat sacrificed by Labour throughout Britain in 1945 was Carmarthen, a highly individualistic constituency, where the Liberal victor was Rhys Hopkin Morris. One of the many achievements of the post-war Labour governments was the creation of a full democracy in Britain for the first time. The Representation of the People Act of 1948 gave effect to the principle of one vote for each adult and swept away the business vote and university vote. The seat lost by the University of Wales was given to Flintshire, and the new constituencies of Caernarfon and Conwy were created to replace the former Caernarfon County and Borough divisions.

Welsh support for the Labour party remained constant at about 58 per cent of the poll in the general elections of 1950, 1951, 1955 and 1959, while its control of the local authorities of industrial Wales became even stronger. By the fifties, the challenge of the Communists had receded and those of the Ratepayers and of Plaid Cymru were at best intermittent, with the result that one-party politics prevailed on the town councils of the coalfield valleys, an arrangement which bred its own problems. On the local councils in rural Wales, on the other hand, party politics (which had been extraordinarily lively in the late nineteenth century) had long since disappeared, and most members were nominally Independents, although many remained Liberal in thought and outlook.

### Aneurin Bevan

He was born in 1897 at Tredegar, Monmouthshire. He was educated at Sirhowy Elementary School until aged thirteen, and read widely about economics, philosophy and politics. He became a miner in 1911, was strongly opposed to the First World War and was elected chairman of the local branch of the South Wales Miners' Federation in 1916. He attended the Central Labour College, London, in 1919–21, returned home to face unemployment and became a member of Tredegar Town Council in 1922. During the 1926 miners' strike he served as a local spokesman, and in 1929 he was elected Labour MP for Ebbw Vale. In the thirties he became a harsh critic of Neville Chamberlain and remained opposed to the government throughout the Second World War. He was chosen as Health Minister in the 1945 Labour Government, laid the foundations of the National Health Service and embarked on a radical programme of slum clearance and the provision of council properties. He remained on the far left of the Labour party throughout the fifties and became the party's deputy leader in 1959. He wrote a large number of pamphlets, articles and the volume *In Place of Fear* (1952). His wife, Jennie Lee, was the Labour MP for North Lanark, 1929–32, and Cannock, 1945–70. He died in 1960.

The Liberal party vote plunged in north and west Wales in post-war elections. Labour won Caernarfonshire in 1945, Pembroke in 1950, Merioneth and Anglesey in 1951, Carmarthen in the 1957 by-election and Cardigan in 1966. In 1959 the Liberals could muster no more than 8 candidates in the whole of Wales and won a derisory 5 per cent of the poll. The spasmodic Liberal 'revivals' which occurred in England and Scotland in the fifties and sixties made little impression upon Wales. Montgomery alone remained true to the Liberals by the late sixties, but even this seat was held by a Conservative from 1979 to 1983.

Labour strength in Wales reached a zenith in 1966 when the party won 32 of the 36 Welsh seats, including all the industrial divisions and all those in Gwynedd, Dyfed, Gwent and Cardiff. Among the Labour MPs from Wales were two successive leaders of the Labour party – James Callaghan (Cardiff South) and Michael Foot (Ebbw Vale) – and George Thomas (Cardiff West) who became Speaker of the House of Commons. Thereafter the Labour party's rule in Wales became less monolithic. Four seats were narrowly lost to the Conservatives in the general election of 1970, and both the Conservatives and Plaid Cymru made further inroads in the two general elections held in 1974.

## The nationalist challenge

Attlee's governments displayed scant interest in devolution, most of their members believing that strong centralized planning was the answer to 'regional' economic problems. A request for a Secretary of State for Wales in 1946 was hastily swept aside by Attlee, and the attitude of Aneurin Bevan, the most influential of the Welsh Labour MPs, towards Welsh questions was at best ambivalent. Plaid Cymru, although much stronger in 1945 than in 1939, remained very much on the periphery of Welsh political life. Yet as Labour expanded its areas of support within Wales, pressure grew to draft policies which would give some institutional recognition to Wales. In 1948 the Council of Wales, under the chairmanship of Huw T. Edwards, was set up, but was given little authority. The Conservative Government elected in 1951 gave the title Minister for Welsh Affairs initially to the Home Secretary and subsequently to the Minister for Housing and Local Government. A Parliament for Wales Campaign was inaugurated by *Undeb Cymru Fydd* in 1949, and presented to Parliament a petition signed by 250,000 Welsh people in 1956, but to no avail. A bill to achieve a Welsh Parliament introduced by S.O. Davies in 1955 suffered a similar fate.

Plaid Cymru, still a small, largely rural movement, made increasing progress during the second half of the 1950s, its new-found support reflected in 20 nationalist candidates in the general election of 1959, when 6 at least retained their deposits. At this election, Labour's manifesto promised the creation of a Welsh Office with a Secretary of State for Wales holding a Cabinet seat. The promise was made good in 1964 and in subsequent years the Welsh Office based at Cardiff (the Welsh capital city since 1955) accumulated a wide range of administrative responsibilities for many aspects of Welsh government. Gwynfor Evans's dramatic and unexpected victory for Plaid Cymru in the Carmarthen by-election of July 1966 (held on the death of Lady Megan Lloyd George) had equally striking repercussions in high, though not winning, numbers of votes in by-elections in industrial constituencies – the Rhondda (1967), Caerphilly (1968) and Merthyr Tydfil (1972), when Labour

*The counties and districts of Wales after local government reorganization in 1974.*

was indeed 'humbled in the very heartland of British socialism'. Even Merthyr Tydfil Town Council came under Plaid Cymru control for a while. Plaid Cymru clearly could muster significant support, if spasmodically, outside the rural areas. By the late sixties some within the councils of the Labour party were anxious to consider a more far-reaching scheme of devolution. Many argued that an elected council for Wales would complement admirably the proposed change in the structure of local government in Wales, an argument reinforced by the government's anxiety to join the European Community. The Crowther Commission on the Constitution was set up in 1969. In the report of the renamed Kilbrandon Commission which appeared in 1973 eleven commissioners supported the idea of an elected assembly for Wales and six voiced support for a legislative parliament.

### James Griffiths

Born in 1890 at Betws, near Ammanford in Carmarthenshire, James Griffiths spent his childhood in a culturally rich and resilient community in the shadow of the religious revival of 1904–5 and of the Independent Labour party. He worked as a coal-miner, spent the years 1919–21 at the Central Labour College, and in 1923 was appointed full-time organizer for the Labour party in the Llanelli constituency. Two years later he became a miners' agent at Burry Port, a post which he held until he entered Parliament as the Labour MP for Llanelli in 1936. He remained in the Commons until his retirement in 1970. He had served as President of the South Wales Miners' Federation in 1934. He held a number of high offices at Westminster, including Minister of National Insurance, 1945–50, Chairman of the Labour party, 1948–9, and Secretary of State for the Colonies, 1950–1. He was responsible for implementing the proposals of the Beveridge Report with measures for national insurance. national assistance and industrial injuries compensation. He was Welsh-speaking, a fervent Welshman, consistently sympathetic to the demands of devolution. He urged that Wales should be treated as a distinct administrative unit in the Attlee Cabinets of 1945–51. He was the first Secretary of State for Wales in 1964–6, responsible for the setting up of the new department. In 1969 he published an autobiography, *Pages from Memory*. He died in 1975.

Plaid Cymru victories in Caernarfon and Merioneth in the general election of February 1974 (followed by success at Carmarthen in October 1974), paralleled by sweeping nationalist triumphs in Scotland, placed Welsh and Scottish devolution firmly on the political agenda. The influence of the nationalists at Westminster increased as the majority of James Callaghan's Labour Government grew ever smaller. The Wales Act reached the Statute Book in July 1978. The powers of the proposed assembly were circumscribed indeed: it was not given the authority to legislate or to raise its own revenue. But to its supporters the proposed assembly represented a signal triumph as an elected body which would serve as a voice for Wales. A building in Cardiff was even selected as the Assembly House. In a referendum held on 1 March 1979, however, eighty per cent of those who voted expressed their opposition to the setting up of the Assembly. Every one of the eight new Welsh counties, even Gwynedd, voted strongly 'No', and Welsh devolution seemed to disappear from the political agenda.

## Local government reorganization

The passage of the Local Government Act of 1972 heralded a sweeping reorganization of Welsh local government which came into effect on 1 April 1974. The boundaries of all the Welsh counties were changed as indeed were their names. There were eight new counties, most of their names derived from the ancient tribal divisions of Wales: Gwynedd in the north-west, Clwyd in the north-east, Powys in mid Wales, Dyfed in the south-west, while Glamorgan was split three ways into West, Mid and South sections, and Monmouthshire alone continued life as the new county of Gwent, its boundaries largely unchanged. Twenty-three of the thirty-seven lower-tier districts were granted borough status, some of these as large as the traditional counties in the rural areas. The new counties were certainly more balanced in terms of population and the units of local government were larger than their predecessors.

By the summer of 1991 attention had begun to focus increasingly on the contentious Welsh Office proposals for local government reform. The suggestion that a single-tier system should be set up was generally welcomed, but opinions diverged wildly on the number and areas of jurisdiction of the proposed new authorities. Eventually it was announced in March 1993 that the eight county and 37 district councils would be replaced by 22 unitary authorities, a change which eventually occurred on 1 April 1996. Almost immediately, however, the apparent weakness of the new authorities attracted vehement criticism.

## Political developments

In 1979 the Labour party's share of the Welsh vote fell from 61 to 45 per cent and it won only 21 seats in Wales. By 1982 the defection of three of its Welsh Members to the Social and Liberal Democrats meant that it could claim only 18 MPs in Wales. It soon became apparent that the revitalized Conservatives were now the major challenge to Labour in Wales rather than Plaid Cymru which had appeared a real threat throughout much of the sixties and seventies. In the election of that year, Conservatives won 31 per cent of the vote and 11 seats in Wales, including 3 gains – Brecon and Radnor and Anglesey from Labour and Montgomery from the Liberals. A junior minister in the Welsh Office boasted that he could drive from the Severn Bridge to Holyhead without leaving Conservative-held territory.

Before the general election of 1983 the parliamentary constituencies were redistributed, and the total number of Welsh divisions thus increased to thirty-eight. Clwyd gained an additional seat in the north-east and the revision of boundaries in the south emphasized the cities of the southern seaboard and the developing coastal plain at the expense of the valleys, thus disrupting solid Labour areas and creating more marginal, balanced constituencies. In 1983, Labour won only 37.5 per cent of the Welsh vote (its lowest proportion since 1919) and 20 seats, while the Conservatives retained 31 per cent and secured 14 seats. The Conservative upsurge appeared to have been consolidated.

By 1987, however, Labour was regaining strength and in the June general election it captured 4 seats – Cardiff West, Newport West, Bridgend and Clwyd South-West – from the Conservatives, increasing its total to 24 and to 45.1 per cent of the vote. The Liberal-SDP alliance retained both Montgomery and Brecon and Radnor, first won in a by-election in July 1985. Sensationally, Plaid Cymru captured Ynys Môn to hold the whole of Gwynedd, but it slipped back still further in industrial areas. The Conservatives held only 8 seats but still won 29.5 per cent of the poll, thus underlining a remarkable stability of Conservative support in Wales.

However, the 1990s witnessed a resurgence in solid traditional support for the Labour party in Wales, a revival anticipated by striking victories in by-elections in Pontypridd and the Vale of Glamorgan during the spring of 1989, and confirmed by Labour successes in all four Welsh seats in the European elections held in June. Peter Walker, the Secretary of State for Wales whose interventionist style had won considerable respect in Wales, survived Margaret Thatcher's Cabinet re-shuffle in the summer of 1989 only to resign for personal reasons early in the following year. His successor was the Welsh-born David Hunt, MP for Wirral, who remained as Secretary of State until May 1993 when he was succeeded by John Redwood, an unexpected choice who adopted a generally abrasive, sometimes pugnacious style. Welsh Office initiatives largely revolved around a loudly trumpeted strategy to revive the valleys of south Wales and to attract increased investment from abroad.

The march of Labour was reflected still further in by-elections in Neath and Monmouth in the spring of 1991 and in a party vote of 49.5 per cent in the general election of April 1992 when it took 27 of the 38 Welsh constituencies. For the fourth time in succession, however, a Conservative government was elected at Westminster. The Liberals lost Brecon and Radnor and, more sensationally, Ceredigion and Pembroke North, where long-serving Liberal MP Geraint Howells was toppled by Cynog Dafis, who fought on the novel joint platform of Plaid Cymru and the Green party. Neil Kinnock, MP for Islwyn, soon resigned as Labour leader and was succeeded by John Smith.

In June 1994 Labour captured all five Welsh seats and 58 per cent of the popular vote in the European elections, while the Conservatives collapsed to third place behind Plaid Cymru. In June 1995, John Redwood's decision to oppose Prime Minister John Major for the party leadership foreshadowed his departure from the Welsh Office and the succession of William Hague, the 34-year-old MP for Richmond in Yorkshire, whose greater responsiveness and affability made him more generally popular in Wales than his predecessor. Following the Conservative defeat in the general election of 1997, Hague succeeded Major as Conservative party leader, and his links with Wales grew closer when he married Welsh-speaking Ffion Jenkins in December 1997. The landslide Labour victory in the May general election was reflected in its successes in 34 of the 40 Welsh constituencies, many of these seats won with substantial majorities. Plaid Cymru and the Liberal Democrats shared the remaining seats and the Conservatives were left without a single MP in Wales.

## Devolution in the 1990s

Alongside the discussion on local government reform in the early 1990s the question of a Welsh Assembly resurfaced after nigh on a decade in abeyance. The initial reaction from the Welsh Office was predictably frosty. However, the ever-increasing domination of the seemingly omnipotent quangos strengthened the argument of the campaigners in favour of a Welsh Assembly, if only as a means of regulating the powers of the Welsh Office. There was widespread criticism that the Tory government was implementing its policies by the use of party sympathizers on almost a hundred unelected quangos, which were regulating £2,100 million or 34 per cent of Welsh Office spending. The Welsh Development Agency was a particular source of contention. Downing Street argued unrelentingly that elected assemblies for Scotland and Wales would simply presage the inevitable break-up of the United Kingdom.

In May 1995 the Labour party had announced its proposals for devolution, although the friction between the new party leader Tony

Blair and the shadow Secretary of State for Wales Ron Davies, the ambitious MP for Caerphilly, apparently increased. In the following month, Tony Blair announced that referenda would precede the establishment of national assemblies for Wales and Scotland. Following the Labour victory in the general election of 1997 and, contrary to press speculation, Ron Davies was appointed Secretary of State for Wales, and in September, on a low turn-out and by the tiniest of majorities, the Welsh electorate voted in favour of a Welsh assembly. Criticism of the conduct of the ballot and unpleasant protracted wrangling over the precise venue of the new assembly persisted into 1998 and to some extent undermined the sense of elation felt the previous September. Eventually it was decided that the National Assembly would be located in Cardiff.

## Welsh society

The population of Wales grew slowly from about 2.5 million in 1945 to 2.75 million by the 1970s. The Welsh became richer materially, both as individuals and as a society, than ever before in their history. Even when allowance is made for the severe inflation of the period, the average Welsh male wage-earner was twice as wealthy in 1978 as in 1946, a prosperity increased even further by the widespread employment of women. This transformation was reflected in much improved living standards: the universal availability of electricity, almost total television ownership, and widespread car and telephone ownership. The sale of consumer durables flourished. The majority came to enjoy comfortable homes (both new buildings and renovated slums), a varied diet and abundant clothing. Even foreign holidays increased hugely in popularity.

### Welsh sport

The public appeal of mass sport has remained strong in Wales throughout the twentieth century, especially in the south. Cricket is a popular summer pastime, with the Glamorgan County team attracting widespread interest, most recently as county champions in 1997. Association football, too, held great appeal in the coastal ports and rural areas, although none of the four Welsh clubs in the Football League – Cardiff, Swansea, Newport (until 1988) and Wrexham – have enjoyed sufficient success to win mass support. Boxing no longer has the appeal which it exercised in the first half of the century, although several boxers, most recently Joe Calzaghe and Barry Jones, won world championship titles. Rugby remains a truly national passion, although the achievements of the national team in the eighties and nineties cannot be compared with those of the teams of the seventies when two half-backs in particular, Barry John and Gareth Edwards, became household names throughout Wales, and the exciting international matches at the Cardiff Arms Park were genuinely national events, a new 'opium of the masses'. Individuals such as Lynn Davies, Colin Jackson, Tanni Grey and Ian Woosnam have all excelled at the highest levels in their respective sports, and there has been an increasing interest in the less traditional 'sports' of snooker and darts.

These changes were paralleled by an enormous increase in public expenditure, especially on health, education and the social services, and on environmental matters such as housing, roads and transport. The foundations of these changes were laid by the post-war Attlee Government, which attempted to give effect to the recommendations of the Beveridge Report of 1942. The jewel in its crown was the establishment of the National Health Service which provided free medical treatment for everyone and brought all the country's hospitals under the wing of the welfare state. Most of the hospitals in Wales had to be rebuilt, the demand for treatment, now that it was free, was heavier than anticipated, and the principle of a free health service was eroded to some extent. New drugs and improved nutrition led to the eradication of tuberculosis and to a drastic drop in the rate of infant mortality. The contraction of the coal industry meant a fall in the number of pit accidents. Yet illness was more common in Wales than in the rest of the United Kingdom, housing standards were lower, and, as the Aberfan disaster of 1966 proved so tragically, the Welsh industrial environment could still pose terrible problems. Moreover, the close-knit community life of the industrial valleys and rural areas was fast disappearing by the seventies. The Welsh work-force was more mobile, more ready to commute, more prepared to inhabit the new-style anonymous housing estates rather than the warm, close rows of terraced houses on the sides and bottoms of the valleys. Official statistics revealed a striking upsurge in the level of reported crime, although increased levels of spending on law and order, the health service and the education system by the new Labour government in 1997 and 1998 appeared to give rise to some greater optimism and hope.

## Education, Language and Culture

The post-war generation also saw a massive expansion of educational horizons. The Butler Education Act of 1944 extended secondary education to everyone and raised the school-leaving age to fifteen. The education authorities provided secondary modern schools for those who failed the eleven-plus examination, but the cost of maintaining a two-tier system proved prohibitive, and some authorities had embraced the comprehensive principle long before Harold Wilson's Labour Government insisted on a comprehensive system in 1964–6. In the wake of the Robbins Report of 1964, the University of Wales also expanded, with mandatory grants for students and an increasing variety in the range of subjects offered. St David's College, Lampeter, and the Science Institute at Cardiff became part of the national University of Wales, which, by 1977–8 had a total of 18,653 students, some ten times as many as in 1939. By the time the University celebrated its centenary in 1992–3, the numbers had increased dramatically to 30,625, with further frenzied expansion in subsequent years.

These changes in government-sponsored education were inevitably accompanied by a decline in the activities of the WEA, the miners' libraries and the welfare halls. Even more striking was the decline in the influence and membership of the chapels, manifested above all in the decay of the Nonconformist ethos, once all-powerful in Welsh life. In 1975, only 6 of the 37 Welsh districts voted to close their public houses on Sundays; by 1989 Dwyfor in

Gwynedd was the only 'dry' district in Wales, and in 1996 even this area voted to conform with the rest of the country.

Welsh-language literary output remained buoyant. The older generation of poets – W.J. Gruffydd, T. Gwynn Jones, T.H. Parry-Williams and R. Williams Parry – was succeeded by some formidable poets, notably D. Gwenallt Jones, Waldo Williams and Euros Bowen. They were followed in the sixties and seventies by poets such as Dic Jones, Bobi Jones, Gwyn Thomas, Bryan Martin Davies and the younger Menna Elfyn, Alan Llwyd and Gerallt Lloyd Owen. Most of these are still productive in the nineties and have been joined by Gwyneth Lewis and Iwan Llwyd. The Welsh short story was given a new lease of life by Kate Roberts, whose sensitive and imaginative portrayals of the quarrying communities of Gwynedd commanded widespread admiration. She also wrote a number of powerful novels, as did T. Rowland Hughes in the forties and Islwyn Ffowc Elis in the fifties and sixties. The nostalgic autobiographical accounts of D.J. Williams have become much-admired classics, and Saunders Lewis's dramas and other writings have proved seminal to the development of the Welsh literary scene. The drama also flourished in the works of John Gwilym Jones and Gwenlyn Parry, and the advent of S4C (the Welsh-language television channel) has inspired greater productivity in this area. Novelists who came to prominence in the sixties and seventies include Jane Edwards, Eigra Lewis Roberts and John Rowlands, while the eighties and nineties have seen the emergence of an exciting new generation of novelists, in particular Aled Islwyn, Robin Llywelyn, Mihangel Morgan, William Owen Roberts and Angharad Tomos.

Such literary activity in the Welsh language was paralleled by the emergence of a new school of Anglo-Welsh writers, writing in English but with their roots firmly in Wales. Caradoc Evans who wrote during and just after the First World War was followed in the thirties by Jack Jones, born in the Rhondda, Idris Davies of Rhymney, Alun Lewis of Aberdare, Vernon Watkins of Swansea and, above all, Dylan Thomas. Later, there came Glyn Jones, Roland Mathias, Raymond Garlick, Raymond Williams and R.S. Thomas, all developing the vigour of the Anglo-Welsh tradition in the pages of an array of dynamic new journals, among them the *Anglo-Welsh Review*, launched in 1958, *Poetry Wales* (1965) and *Planet* (1970). The writers who came to prominence in the sixties and seventies included novelists Emyr Humphreys and Raymond Williams, and poets Dannie Abse, Harri Webb, John Tripp and Gillian Clarke. The younger generation writing in the eighties and nineties has shown an ability to take traditional themes into new directions and has produced some striking novels by Christopher Meredith and Duncan Bush, the forceful theatre of Ed Thomas, and the poetry of Robert Minhinnick and Tony Curtis.

## Dylan Thomas

He was born in 1914 at Swansea where his father was an English master. He was educated at Swansea Grammar School and became a reporter on the *South Wales Daily Post*, his only period of full-time employment. Between 1934 and 1939 he published three volumes of poetry steeped in an atmosphere of adolescence and an intense sexual assertiveness, and contributed reviews to distinguished periodicals such as *New Verse* and *The Adelphi*. In 1937 he married Caitlin Macnamara and soon moved to Laugharne in Carmarthenshire, publishing in 1940 a volume of autobiographical short stories, *Portrait of the Artist as a Young Dog*. During the Second World War, he wrote a number of radio and film scripts and participated in broadcast talks and readings. His life alternated between rural Wales and proximity to London, made necessary by his film and radio work. The late 1940s saw the publication of a spate of poetry, his return to live in the Boat House at Laugharne in 1949, and a number of lucrative lecture tours of the USA. His famous 'play of voices', *Under Milk Wood*, occupied most of his attention from 1950, but new poems were also written during the last years of his life. His heavy drinking and financial irresponsibility took their toll, and Thomas died in New York in November 1953. His body lies buried in the churchyard at Laugharne, while a memorial stone was placed in Poets' Corner in Westminster Abbey in 1982.

## Welsh music

Music in Wales has continued to flourish in various ways. The National Eisteddfod has provided a powerful fillip to choral singing, although male-voice choirs, while popular, do not flourish as they did before 1914. Welsh music has had a wider impact through the export of leading Welsh singers, such as the late Sir Geraint Evans, Dame Gwyneth Jones and, more recently, Bryn Terfel to the opera houses of Covent Garden and La Scala, and the Welsh National Orchestra also made a major contribution in this area. The Welsh National Opera Company, set up in 1946, continues to enjoy a fine international reputation. Native composers such as Alun Hoddinott and William Mathias have produced work reflecting an intense Welsh consciousness and sense of cultural identity. On a more popular level the sixties and seventies saw singers such as Tom Jones and Shirley Bassey achieve international renown, while the nineties have seen the emergence of top groups such as Catatonia, Manic Street Preachers, Stereophonics and Super Furry Animals.

The Welsh language and culture were visibly under threat by the third quarter of the twentieth century, as indeed was the distinctive English-language culture of the south Wales valleys. By 1971 fewer than one-fifth of the Welsh people could speak their native tongue, and the 1981 census revealed Gwynedd to be the only county with a majority of Welsh-speakers. Few communities survived where Welsh remained the natural medium of communication for all activities. The language was increasingly under threat from a continuing inward migration from English cities, especially of retired people, to rural areas, many of which also contained a significant number of 'second' or 'holiday' homes. The sharp influx of more than 40,000 into the three countries of Dyfed, Gwynedd and Powys during the 1980s no doubt contributed to the unemployment problem. Ceredigion alone saw a net increase of 9,000 in its population, the highest proportion of immigrants in the whole of the United Kingdom, counterbalanced by a steady drift away from the depressed industrial valleys of south Wales. The resultant mixed population in rural Wales inevitably led to persistent wrangling over the teaching of Welsh in rural schools, most notably in Dyfed.

Yet there are grounds for optimism. The number speaking the language has remained fairly constant in some of the most Welsh communities, while in some primarily English areas there are more young people than middle-aged people able to speak Welsh. Strenuous efforts have been made to save the language, especially within the education system. A Welsh school sponsored by *Urdd Gobaith Cymru* (the Welsh League of Youth, founded in 1922) opened its doors at Aberystwyth in 1939, followed by a Welsh school at Llanelli, controlled by Carmarthenshire Local Education Authority, in 1947. By 1974 there were 61 designated Welsh primary schools educating 8,500 pupils. The first secondary schools to teach largely through the medium of Welsh were established in Flintshire in 1956 (Ysgol Glan Clwyd) and in 1961 (Ysgol Maes Garmon), followed by Rhydfelen near Pontypridd in 1962. By the mid-1980s there were fifteen such schools, as well as a number of non-designated schools where some subjects were offered through the medium of Welsh. By the time the 1991 census was taken there was an encouraging increase in the number of schoolchildren able to speak the Welsh language. Teaching through the medium of Welsh has also increased within the University.

Although many Welsh-language journals have disappeared, others have survived through government grants, which have also sustained the Welsh book trade and indeed the National Eisteddfod. On the other hand, the most exciting development of the seventies, the *papurau bro* (community newspapers), began life spontaneously quite independent of government support, and by 1992 it was estimated that there were some fifty of these papers in Wales. The activities of *Cymdeithas yr Iaith Gymraeg*, founded in 1962, have greatly enhanced the status of the language, primarily perhaps in the world of television, culminating in the reluctant granting in 1982 of a fourth television channel to be devoted to Welsh-language programmes. The number of hours of Welsh-language broadcasting has steadily increased on both television and radio. The Welsh Language Board, whose main function is 'to promote and facilitate the use of the Welsh language', came into being in 1993 with Lord Elis-Thomas, the former Plaid Cymru MP for Merioneth Nant Conwy, as its first chairman.

# 11

# Wales in the New Millennium

## *Welsh political life*

During the 1997 Welsh devolution campaign, Ron Davies, the Secretary of State for Wales and the Labour MP for Caerphilly, had asserted that 'through the Welsh National Assembly we can create a country that more fully embodies the values of social justice and equality which have long animated the people of Wales'. Following the outcome of the 1997 poll, Davies, a convert to devolutionary initiatives, had commented with typical perspicacity, 'Let no one think that now the devolution genie is out of his bottle he can be forced back in or that he won't want to stretch his muscles'. He had always insisted that 'devolution was a process rather than an event'. The extremely narrow 'Yes' vote then saw several Welsh towns and cities – among them Swansea, Aberystwyth, Wrexham and even Machynlleth – vying to be the venue of the new assembly but, ultimately and predictably, it was the Welsh capital city Cardiff that won the day as the seat of the 60-member new National Assembly for Wales. A temporary home at Crickhowell House later gave way to an impressive glass, slate and steel building designed by the Richard Rogers Partnership and officially opened by Queen Elizabeth II on St David's Day 2006 – named the 'Senedd', an appellation (*senedd* means *parliament*) which seemed to suggest that a more far-reaching devolution of powers was imminent. The Senedd building soon won prestigious awards for both its sustainability and its green credentials.

One previously unforeseen result of devolution was to weaken the vice-like grip of the Labour Party upon Welsh national life. Long before this, very few of the party's MPs had come from a manual worker background. The first National Assembly for Wales elections were held on 6 May 1999, a century after the death of the devolution pioneer Thomas Edward Ellis MP. The overall turnout of voters was 46.3 per cent, considered disappointingly low by commentators. Out of a total of 60 Assembly Members (40 directly elected by the Welsh constituencies, and 20 on the regional lists), there were 28 Labour, 17 Plaid Cymru, 9 Conservative and 6 Liberal Democrat AMs. Although the Welsh Labour Party thus had the biggest representation, they did not gain enough seats to form a majority government (in part because of the application of proportional representation), and subsequently entered into a coalition with the Liberal Democrats, led in the Assembly by Mike German (who then became Deputy First Minister), in October 2000.

The election was marked by the historically high level of support for Plaid Cymru, who had won their highest share of the vote in any Wales-wide election. The party won considerable support in such traditionally safe Labour areas as the valleys of south Wales, dramatically capturing the Rhondda and Islwyn constituencies, and also winning Conwy, Carmarthen East and Dinefwr, and Llanelli, only narrowly failing to win several other seats. These sensational successes were largely attributed to the inspiring party leadership of Dafydd Wigley and, in the Labour camp, the somewhat insecure position of Alun Michael who had succeeded the strongly pro-devolutionist Ron Davies as Secretary of State for Wales. Generally, in the new age of devolution, as more powers were transferred to the European Union, Plaid Cymru, emboldened by its success in Assembly elections, tended to backtrack somewhat from its long-term policy of securing for Wales the status of an independent nation state, and pressed for Wales to become a member state of the EU just like the United Kingdom.

From the outset of its existence there were insistent gibes (which continue to this very day) that the new body was little more than a glorified county council sitting in the Welsh capital, while its range of powers seemed very limited and conspicuously far less extensive than those granted to the Scottish Parliament at

Edinburgh. The Assembly seemed totally unable, for example, to influence the decision of multinational companies to close down factory plants in Wales – these included the closure of the plant owned by the steel company Corus in Ebbw Vale. Nor did the Assembly enjoy very much success in its efforts to redistribute wealth more equitably to the regions of Wales. The affluent areas of Wales, particularly along and to the south of the M4 corridor between Chepstow and Bridgend, and the A55 expressway traversing north Wales and which enjoyed a close proximity to the motorways of north-west England linking to Manchester airport, seemed positively light years removed from the depression hit valleys of the former south Wales coalfield – although, geographically, these were only a short distance removed from the more prosperous regions.

The early years of the National Assembly were dominated by intense bickering over the readiness of the British Government to pay its share of the cost of implementing Objective One, which was a recognition by the EEC that the old coalfield valleys of south Wales and the rural areas of the western hinterland alike were among the most deprived areas in the whole of western Europe. It was considered essential that increased resources be channelled into strengthening the economic, social and cultural life of these areas; already, in 1998, the EEC had earmarked £1.2 billion for this task, assuming that the UK government at Westminster would also contribute a similar sum for this purpose. But the UK treasury proved reluctant to part with its cash, and the efforts of Alun Michael to persuade it to loosen its purse strings seemed to fall on stubbornly deaf ears.

Alun Michael, widely considered to be little more than a stopgap Blairite placeman, was regarded as generally uninspiring by his colleagues and was frequently the butt of cruel gibes by opposition politicians. In February 2000, he was replaced by the more gregarious, affable, heavyweight presence of Rhodri Morgan, who became known as the 'First Minister' (*Prif Weinidog* in Welsh) of the National Assembly. Morgan, the Labour MP for Cardiff West since 1987, had a track record of unwavering support for devolution, and he now

*The Debating Chamber at the National Assembly for Wales*

sought to impose a distinctively Welsh form of democratic socialism in the National Assembly, which he rightly depicted as 'a fragile flower'. Other changes of personnel were also afoot. In August 1999, Nick Bourne had succeeded Rod Richards as the leader of the Conservative group in the Assembly and, in May 2000, serious health and family issues propelled Plaid Cymru leader Dafydd Wigley into yielding his place to Ieuan Wyn Jones. Distinctive ultra-generous policies were implemented in relation to medical prescriptions, tests for school pupils and student fees, but it was widely felt that the ambit of the Assembly's activities was largely confined to more peripheral matters, the result of its severely curtailed powers and a possible lack of imagination and political will by its leadership.

There was a popular perception in Wales that the UK parliament remained much more crucial politically than the Senedd in Cardiff Bay – reflected in a creditable turnout of 61.4 per cent in the May 2001 general election at which the highly marginal Ynys Môn fell to the Labour Party's Albert Owen, and Carmarthen East and Dinefwr was won by Adam Price, Plaid Cymru's most able rising star. Generally, the novel policies advocated by Tony Blair and 'New Labour' found but little support among Welsh traditional 'Old Labour' supporters in the valleys; many Labour supporters in Wales looked askance at the attack on Iraq, with several Labour MPs from Wales voting against the move in the House of Commons.

In the second National Assembly elections, convened on 1 May 2003, turnout fell to a paltry 38.18 per cent, and there was witnessed some resurgence for the Welsh Labour Party, which won 30 seats, while Plaid Cymru (now suffering severely from the withdrawal from the National Assembly of political heavyweights like Dafydd Wigley, Phil Williams and Cynog Dafis) saw a reduction in support, winning just 12 seats. There were, in addition, 11 Conservative and 6 Liberal Democrat AMs. There now appeared to be some restoration of the Conservatives to Welsh national life, although the party had no MPs representing Wales at Westminster. This election also saw the return of former Labour MP John Marek, representing the Wrexham constituency, as an independent member in the Assembly.

With his party having won exactly half the total seats in the Assembly, Rhodri Morgan, the Labour First Minister, chose to govern without a coalition partner and formed a unique administration with an equal number of men and women members –proportionally at that time the highest women's representation anywhere in the world. But the government was manifestly precarious as the opposition parties between them could muster the remaining 30 votes. Difficulties increased still further when Peter Law, the Labour AM for Blaenau Gwent, resigned from his party in protest against its decision to select general election candidates from shortlists comprising women only – a pointed attempt to improve the gender imbalance in the Labour Party and in parliament. When Law then re-captured Blaenau Gwent as an independent, the Labour Party forfeited what had perhaps been its safest Welsh seat.

The new administration set up the Richard Commission to examine the responsibilities and the future development of the National Assembly. Its report, published in March 2004, proposed that in due course the Assembly should have legislative powers, that its membership should be increased to eighty, elected by the single transferable vote, and that these changes should be implemented by the year 2011. A few months later, the Assembly made a spirited attempt to tackle the problem of the quangos. The need for 'a bonfire of the quangos' had been frequently advanced during the various devolution campaigns; in July 2004, it was announced that the Welsh Development Agency, the Wales Tourist Board and Learning Wales would become subject to the control of the National Assembly, soon to be followed by the Arts Council of Wales and the recently established Welsh Language Board (with much concern expressed in particular about political interference in the affairs of the latter).

Devolution was hardly mentioned at all during the general election campaign of May 2005, when 29 Welsh seats were won by Labour, 4 by the Liberal Democrats (who now captured Cardiff Central, a real breakthrough for the party, and Ceredigion), 3 by Plaid Cymru, 3 by the Conservatives (something of a Welsh comeback for them), and one by an independent candidate, namely

Peter Law in Blaenau Gwent. When Law sadly died the following year, his Assembly seat was retained by his widow Trish, and his Westminster seat was taken by his agent Dai Davies. 'New Labour' ideals still seemed generally unpopular in much of Wales.

The UK government White Paper, *Better Government for Wales*, published in June 2005, was generally critical of the recommendations of the Richard Report, proposing a cautious middle course between the status quo and enhanced legislative powers broadly similar to those currently exercised by the Scottish Parliament. On his first visit to Wales as Leader of the Opposition during the following December, David Cameron stated that 'devolution is here to stay'. The Government of Wales Act 2006 then reformed the National Assembly and allowed further powers to be more easily granted. The Act created a system of government with a separate executive drawn from, and accountable to, the legislature. It created an executive body – the Welsh Assembly Government (and known since May 2011 as the Welsh Government) – that is separate from the legislative body, that is, the National Assembly for Wales. There were many critics who argued that this concession was no more than plain subterfuge. The journalist Martin Shipton asserted, 'We remain as subservient as we ever were to the Westminster parliament. The devolution settlement imposed on Wales by the Government of Wales Act of 2006 amounts to nothing more than a conjuring trick designed to conceal an instrument of national humiliation.' Even so, it could not be denied that the National Assembly had made its mark on the world scene, in part as a result of its number of women AMs, which made up fully one-half of the assembly membership, an unprecedented composition worldwide.

In the third National Assembly elections held in May 2007, Plaid Cymru made gains at the expense of the Labour Party, although Labour, with 26 AMs, still remained the largest party in the Assembly, as they had been ever since its inception. There were now 15 Plaid Cymru, 12 Conservative and 6 Liberal Democrat AMs. Plaid Cymru stated it would make a referendum on the devolving of further powers to the National Assembly a condition for any coalition. It was reported that senior civil servants before the election were preparing for three possible coalition administrations: Labour/ Liberal Democrat, Labour/Plaid Cymru or Plaid Cymru/Liberal Democrat/Conservative. Discussions between Plaid Cymru, the Conservatives and the Liberal Democrats to form a 'rainbow' coalition broke down, and a coalition was eventually agreed between Labour and Plaid Cymru, an unlikely scenario of traditional political enemies now joining forces, and the new coalition came into being on 7 July 2007. It drew up an agreement called 'One Wales', which committed the administration to supporting moves towards a Welsh parliament with full law-making powers.

It soon became clear that Labour politicians in the Assembly, led by Rhodri Morgan, were pursuing policies which stood in clear contradistinction to those implemented by the Labour government at Westminster. Morgan insisted that clear-cut 'clear red water' now separated Cardiff and London. The distinctive, innovative policies implemented in Wales included free medical prescriptions for all, free bus passes for the over-60s, free entry to museums and art galleries, the abolition of health trusts, a total ban on smoking in all public places, the abolition of school league tables, and new ways of supporting the higher education sector in Wales. The last named initiative has extended in recent years to subsidising heavily the fees of students from Wales in all higher education institutions, a colossally expensive commitment in itself. A Children's Commissioner was appointed, followed by a Commissioner for the Elderly. Some of these worthy initiatives in Wales were later emulated by central government at Westminster.

In the 'One Wales' coalition agreement on 27 June 2007, the Wales Labour Party and Plaid Cymru made the commitment 'to proceed to a successful outcome of a referendum for full law-making powers under Part IV of the Government of Wales 2006 as soon as practicable, at or before the end of the Assembly term'. The two parties agreed 'in good faith to campaign for a successful outcome to such a referendum', and to set up an All Wales Convention to prepare for such a successful outcome. In November 2009, a report by the All Wales Convention found that public opinion was narrowly in favour of increasing the powers of the Welsh Assembly.

A referendum on extending the law-making powers of the National Assembly for Wales was held in Wales on 3 March 2011. The referendum asked the question, 'Do you want the Assembly now to be able to make laws on *all* matters in the twenty subject areas it has powers for?' These included health, education, culture and economic development. If a majority voted 'yes', the Assembly would then be able to make laws, known as Acts of the Assembly, on all matters in the subject areas, without needing the agreement of the UK parliament. If a majority voted 'no', the arrangements in place at the time of the referendum would have continued – that is, in each devolved area, the Assembly would be able to make its own laws on some matters, but not others. To make laws on any of these other matters, the Assembly would have had to ask the UK parliament to transfer the powers to it. The results of the referendum were announced on 4 March 2011. Overall, 63.49 per cent voted 'yes', and 36.51 per cent voted 'no'. In 21 of 22 local authorities the vote was 'yes', the exception being Monmouthshire by a very slim majority. The overall turnout, however, was still a paltry 35.2 per cent. Carwyn Jones, the First Minister, in welcoming the positive result, said, 'From the coast to the border, the north to the south, our country is united ... Today an old nation came of age.' In November 2012 the National Assembly for Wales (Official Languages Act) received the Royal Assent. It was the first act passed in Wales to become law in over six hundred years, and was also the first bill passed by the Welsh Assembly since it acquired direct law-making powers in March the previous year. The bill gave the Welsh and English languages equal status within the Assembly. The very same month, the Silk Commission recommended that the Welsh Government should have the power to vary income tax in Wales by the year 2020.

Meanwhile, in the general election held on 6 May 2010, following some evidence of Labour decline and public opposition after its unprecedented thirteen years of office, there were questions over whether perceived Labour 'one-partyism' in Wales would be finally superseded. In fact, the Labour Party remained the party with the greatest representation in Wales, but it did suffer a net loss of 4 seats and its share of the vote dropped by 6.5 per cent; its dominance in the Welsh party system was basically preserved. The Conservatives increased their number of seats by 5, something of a resurgence for them, and the Liberal Democrats and Plaid Cymru saw little change both in the number of seats and their share of the vote. The election in Wales was primarily notable for the Labour Party holding on to its dominant position in Westminster elections despite very adverse circumstances and a historic drop in vote share.

Rather a contrary trend was observed in the 2011 National Assembly elections. The election resulted in 4 gains for the incumbent Welsh Labour Party, which now has 30 seats, exactly half of the Assembly. The party also secured a swing in its favour of over 10 percentage points. The Welsh Conservatives emerged as the largest opposition party with 14 seats, a net gain of two, but party leader Nick Bourne lost his seat. The junior party in the previous government coalition, Plaid Cymru, suffered a drop in its vote and lost 4 seats. The Welsh Liberal Democrats also lost significantly in the popular vote and returned 5 AMs, having lost one. Plaid Cymru then shared a platform with the SNP in seeking to stand up for Wales and Scotland against the expected expenditure cuts of David Cameron's coalition government. During 2013–14, devolution was firmly back on the political agenda because of the impending referendum on Scottish independence and the disparate reactions to its prospects and potential benefits.

## Welsh Society

The 2001 census revealed that Wales had a population of 2.9 million individuals, almost half of them resident in the Cardiff commuter belt, and fully 18 per cent over 65 years of age. Colwyn Bay was the only town of any substantial size in the rural areas. Almost one-quarter of the population had been born outside Wales. Great concern was expressed that many Welsh communities were becoming dominated by increasing numbers of English migrants, very few of whom made any real effort to learn and speak the Welsh language. Second and holiday homes in rural Wales remained a thorny issue as house prices were being driven relentlessly ever upwards beyond the reach of local people on modest incomes.

Economic and industrial fortunes were very mixed. The northeast benefited considerably as a result of the decision of the British Steel Corporation to set up the Deeside Industrial Park which soon became home to a large number of factories. Other beneficial initiatives included the arrival of Toyota, the expansion of the Broughton plant of British Aerospace and the massive Ford plant based at Bridgend, and the setting up of new initiatives like Bosch at Pontyclun and Inmos at Newport. But elsewhere in Wales depression was endemic, living standards poor and unemployment levels high – both in the valleys of the south and the rural areas of the west and north. Wage levels varied dramatically in different parts of the country and insistent demands arose that Wales would be a most worthy recipient of Objective One funding.

Wales had a relatively high proportion of pensioners, incapacity benefit was being claimed by escalating numbers of recipients, and there was a visible paucity of well-paid, professional posts, a tendency intensified by the increasing employment of women who tended to earn lower salaries than men. The marked, severe contraction of the once dominant coal and steel industries had exercised a profound effect on the lopsided Welsh economy. Rural Wales, too, had its share of problems – an over-dependence on governmental subsidies for farmers, the continuation of strict milk quotas, the impact of diseases like BSE and foot and mouth, and the continuing acceleration of amalgamating farms to form much larger units. The small-scale Welsh family farm was rapidly becoming a thing of the past. By 2001, only 1.07 per cent of the Welsh workforce was employed in agriculture (compared with 4.5 per cent back in 1971). One result was the ever increasing numbers of 'adventitious rural dwellers' in parts of Wales, people who lived there simply because they liked the area rather than because of any economic or occupational necessity.

While the city of Cardiff developed at breakneck speed, chill economic winds blew over so much of the rest of Wales, which remained a land of glaring contradictions. Indeed, a UK governmental survey undertaken at the beginning of 2007 established that eight of the top ten 'unhealthiest places to live' in the UK were in Wales, with Merthyr Tydfil heading the list. January 2008 saw the final closure of the Tower colliery, Hirwaun, the last deep mine in the south Wales valleys, and one owned and run since 1995 by the miners themselves using their NCB redundancy payments – a deeply symbolic event. Government statistics released in March 2010 revealed that the unemployment rate in Wales, at 9.2 per cent, was higher than in any other home nation, and higher than all but two other regions of the United Kingdom. The results of a survey by the prominent charity Save the Children published in February 2011 revealed that no fewer than one in seven children in Wales was being brought up in severe poverty. 'Child poverty in Wales exposed as UK's worst', ran the striking headline in the *Western Mail*.

The harsh public spending cuts imposed by David Cameron's coalition government elected in 2010 inevitably led to substantial job losses in Wales as elsewhere, but the recession of the 2010s, although severe, still did not replicate the intense deprivation and primary poverty experienced during the interwar years. Formidable problems remain to blight Wales. Her manufacturing base has shrunk, possibly irretrievably; its birthrate continues to decline; house prices still spiral out of control in some areas; and serious health problems remain. European grant support and the block grants from London, controlled by the loathed Barnett formula, are generally inadequate to revive ailing fortunes in Wales.

Social and communal life has been increasingly transformed in the twenty-first century by ever growing computer ownership and ever increasing access to, and use of, the Internet and the web, which have completely transformed information technology in Wales as elsewhere. With the proliferation of satellite and digital technology, people in Wales now have access to positively scores, potentially even hundreds, of various television channels. In 2004, ITV Wales succeeded HTV, while S4C had launched its own digital channel back in 1998 with no fewer than twelve full hours of broadcasting per day. A deal struck between the BBC and S4C in January 2013 has ensured independent Welsh language broadcasting, funded by the BBC licence fee, until at least 2017. The numbers of local radio stations has multiplied rapidly too, fuelled in particular by the ever escalating demand for popular music in Wales as elsewhere.

There have been significant developments in other aspects of Welsh cultural life. Welsh national bands, choirs and orchestras have increased in number and prospered. The Welsh National Opera has gone from strength to strength, acquiring a magnificent new home with the opening of the splendid Millennium Centre in Cardiff Bay in November 2004. Designed by Jonathan Adams, this signature building housed the 2,000-seat Donald Gordon Theatre and several other impressive arts facilities. It was soon to become one of the most impressive and lively performing arts centres in the whole of Europe. Welsh musical genius was exported to all parts of the world by, first and foremost, Bryn Terfel, while Welsh drama was championed by the unique productive genius of Ed Thomas. Two soprano singers – Charlotte Church (who reached number one in the record charts when she was just twelve years of age) and Katherine Jenkins, an outstanding practitioner of classical and sacred music – became major media celebrities. The year 2004 saw the revamped revival of the Welsh Theatre Company and Cwmni Theatr Cymru, both of which sought, generally successfully, to commission high calibre, original work rather than the construction of grand theatre buildings in the tradition of their early twentieth-century heyday. Several talented actors have continued to make their distinctive mark globally, among them Anthony Hopkins, Catherine Zeta Jones, Ioan Gruffudd, Rhys Ifans and Matthew Rhys. An especially iconic event was the decision by the famous Hollywood actor Michael Sheen to return home to his native Port Talbot to act in *The Passion* in 2011. There have been also significant Welsh dimensions to the world of film, highlighted by the published work of Dave Berry, and in the sphere of art championed by the pioneering research of Peter Lord, and reflected in the increasing number of art galleries in Wales. The ownership of a painting by Kyffin Williams became, and still remains, a symbol of well and truly 'having arrived' in certain middle-class Welsh circles, the result of the outlay of several thousand pounds in many cases.

There have been some remarkable Welsh buildings too, some fashioned by the insistent demands of the ecology movement. Edifices of especial distinction include the magnificent Millennium Stadium (the successor to the Cardiff Arms Park, which dated back to 1970, and was completed for the staging of the rugby World Cup in 2000); the Senedd building in Cardiff; the marina at Penarth; and Swansea's maritime district, where the intense popularity of Dylan Thomas shows no sign of diminution to the present day. In October 2009, the St David's Centre in Cardiff re-opened as one of the largest shopping centres in the whole of the United Kingdom after its multi-million pound extension and the reconstruction of the surrounding area.

The long-awaited publication of the 2011 census revealed that the resident population of Wales was now a record high 3.1 million, a 5 per cent increase since 2001. Nearly one in five (18 per cent, 563,000) of residents were aged 65 or over. Wales had a high percentage of residents with a long term health problem or disability, just under a quarter (23 per cent, 696,000) – higher than any region of England. Much concern was soon expressed at the revelation that the group of people aged three and over who could speak, read and write Welsh had decreased one percentage point from 16 per cent (458,000) in 2001 to 15 per cent (431,000) in 2011. It was strikingly significant, too, that the old industrial areas of the southern coalfield contained a significantly higher proportion of Welsh-born people than either Gwynedd or the counties of south-west Wales. In 2011, intriguingly, more households in Wales (67 per cent, 879,000) owned their accommodation than in England (63 per cent, 14.0 million). The number of cars and vans available to households in Wales had also increased from 1.3 to 1.6 million between 2001 and 2011. Nearly all households in Wales reported that they had central heating in 2011 (98 per cent, 1.3 million).

## Welsh Language and Culture

The prowess of Dylan Thomas was emulated primarily by the talented and prolific, if eccentric R. S. Thomas, followed by Gillian Clarke and Gwyneth Lewis – the latter, writing equally proficiently in both Welsh and English, became Wales's first national poet in 2005; Lewis is also an accomplished prose writer. She was succeeded by Gwyn Thomas as national poet in 2006. Their work was paralleled by distinguished Welsh language poets like the late Iwan Llwyd, Myrddin ap Dafydd, Mererid Hopwood and Menna Elfyn. The popularity of *cynghanedd* continues unabated. Prominent younger novelists, with a surreal cutting edge to their work, include the prolific Mihangel Morgan and Robin Llywelyn. Literary output in the Welsh language is still substantial and varied, stimulated by the continued popularity of the National Eisteddfod and the annual youth eisteddfodau of Urdd Gobaith Cymru. The recent election in 2012 by the members of *Gorsedd Beirdd Ynys Prydein* of Swansea University Welsh lecturer Dr Christine James as the first female archdruid of Wales seems to symbolize that the Gorsedd, too, has fully entered into the spirit and ethos of the twenty-first century; Dr James, who was installed in the role in June 2013, is also the first ever Welsh learner to occupy the position. The Llangollen-based International Eisteddfod continues to bring together accomplished performers from all around the globe.

The 2001 census revealed that 575,640 individuals (20.5 per cent of the population of Wales) were able to speak the Welsh language. An additional 222,226 (7.9 per cent) claimed to have some understanding of their mother tongue. These were encouraging indices for advocates of the language, although it was a cause for concern that there was some fall in the number of Welsh speakers in the traditional Welsh heartlands of Anglesey, Gwynedd, Ceredigion and Carmarthenshire alike. The in-migration of English people was counterbalanced by the out-migration of a local population, caused by the lack of employment opportunities in their home areas. Caernarfon, where fully 87.2 per cent of the inhabitants were Welsh-speaking, was the most Welsh town in the whole of Wales.

Welsh language road and directional signs abound (including striking bilingual guiding in the supermarkets of Wales and fully bilingual instructions and announcements at many Welsh railway stations), large numbers of Welsh speakers have flocked to be employed in the media (thus creating what has proved to be a dynamic Welsh media industry), and Wales has its own distinctive education system, now devolved to the control of the National Assembly and run by HEFCW. The provision for Welsh language teaching has increased dramatically. In the 2001 census, 71.9 per cent of the population of Wales claimed to be nominally 'Christian' believers, but the numbers actually attending church and chapel services have plummeted relentlessly throughout Wales, attracted by the compelling appeal of a wide range of other leisure and recreational pursuits, not least the holding of Sunday sporting events. Many once vibrant Nonconformist chapels have closed their doors, others are moribund; yet very few Welsh people declared themselves avowed agnostics or atheists.

*Cardiff's Millennium Stadium*

Rugby, football and cricket continue their dominance of Welsh sporting life, closely followed by the lasting appeal of indoor pursuits like snooker and darts and indeed bowls, which flourishes both on outside greens and in indoor stadia and leisure centres. When the soccer giant John Charles died in 2004, there was an immense outpouring of profound grief throughout Wales. There have been several indices of the resurgence of the Welsh sporting prowess during the last decade or so. In 2005, Wales beat England, Scotland, Ireland, France and Italy to win the Six Nations Rugby Grand Slam for the first time in far too many years. In 2008, record numbers of Welsh sportsmen and women won Olympic and Paralympic Gold medals in Beijing. Glamorgan's Sophia Gardens held the Ashes Test match between England and Australia cricket teams for the first time in 2009, and in the following year the Ryder Cup came to Wales for the first time, with the prestigious golfing event taking place at the Celtic Manor Resort in Newport.

The concept of a distinctive sense of Welsh nationhood is one which has been keenly debated in the Wales of the early twenty-first century, stimulated by the election of the first National Assembly, and the existence of such buildings as St David's Hall, the magnificent Millennium Stadium opened back in 1999 (with a seating capacity for 74,500 people and the first stadium in the UK to feature a retractable roof), the Wales Millennium Centre which adorns Cardiff Bay, and the National Botanic Garden of Wales, opened at Llanarthney in the Towy valley, Carmarthenshire, in May 2000. The National Waterfront Museum in Swansea has also represented a substantial adornment for that city. The National Library has continued to flourish, establishing the Screen and Sound Archive of Wales and the Welsh Political Archive, and exhibiting an ever increasing commitment to digitize its core collections, rendering possible remote access from anywhere to so many of its treasures. Immense resources have been committed to this urgent task. Possibly the only real blot is the apparent near-collapse during recent years of the federal University of Wales, once – ever since 1893 in fact – a deeply revered symbol of Welsh national distinctiveness. One by one, its constituent colleges, led by Cardiff, have assertively broken away and sought greater autonomy and independent degree-awarding powers. The uneasy merger between St Davids University College in Lampeter and Trinity College in Carmarthen has proved to be fraught with setbacks and pitfalls.

The new sense of Welsh national distinctiveness was strikingly demonstrated in 2007 at the funeral at Llanelli's Stradey Park of international rugby star Ray Gravell, also a popular broadcaster and actor, when literally thousands of mourners paid their respects to an iconic figure in a unique commemoration. It seemed that an increasing proportion of the Welsh populace now views itself as distinctively Welsh and is proud of its national institutions. Yet there persists, too, a lingering sense of innate Britishness, encouraged by the pervasive influence of British (usually London-based) broadcasting and newspapers, and the persistence of a deeply embedded sense of royalism (in spite of some staunch republican support too). Indeed, Wales applied for more permits to hold street parties to celebrate the marriage of Prince William to Kate Middleton in June 2011 than any other part of the United Kingdom except London, and there was similar popular enthusiasm in Wales for the Queen's diamond jubilee festivities the following year. In April 2012, the Queen undertook a two-day visit to Wales as part of her diamond jubilee tour; the communities visited over the Welsh section of her tour included Cardiff, Llandaff, Merthyr Tydfil, Aberfan, Ebbw Vale and Crickhowell. Wales is indeed a land of striking contrasts and contradictions. In 2012 the popular broadcaster and writer Jon Gower depicted Wales as a nation 'where economic poverty and cultural ambition sit cheek by jowl ... There are nowadays three million individual stories in Wales, each unique but collectively arresting'.

## Scholarship and Literature

There is cause for pride, too, in Welsh scholarship and publication. *The Oxford Companion to the Literature of Wales*, a massive reference work updated in 1998, has been well received and has stood the test of time. 'Welsh Biography on-line', the successor to the published *Dictionary of Welsh Biography*, with regular additions to its accessible database and edited until recently by Brynley F. Roberts, now flourishes under the auspices of the Centre for Advanced Welsh and Celtic Studies at Aberystwyth, in itself a magisterial research institution which, employing teams of dedicated scholars, has spawned several magnificent series of publications on the language, literature and history of Wales. The recent publication of a magisterial volume by Thomas Charles Edwards, *Wales and the Britons, 350–1064* (2012), means that five of the six projected volumes in the Oxford History of Wales series, launched back in the 1970s, are now available in print. The whole of Wales is by now covered by the six fine volumes of the Pevsner series to *The Buildings of Wales* with their authoritative, minutely researched and checked entries. The Royal Commission on Ancient and Historical Monuments in Wales, based at Aberystwyth, continues to execute its duties with exemplary professionalism, and has also published a spate of important published works.

Welsh history, as an academic discipline and popular pastime, has continued to flourish as never before – in spite of a severe contraction in the provision made for the subject within the university sector. John Davies's brilliantly comprehensive and authoritative single-volume *A History of Wales*, originally published in English in 1990 and in Welsh in 1993, was substantially revised and updated in both languages in fine new, eminently readable, paperback editions available in print in 2007. A little earlier, another distinguished Welsh historian Geraint H. Jenkins published his slimmer *A Concise History of Wales* (2006) for the Cambridge Concise Histories series. Important biographical works include the comprehensive study *Llywelyn ap Gruffudd, Prince of Wales*, by J. Beverley Smith, published in Welsh in 1986 and in English in 1998, and a typically incisive study on *The Revolt of Owain Glyn Dŵr* by the late R. Rees Davies in 1995. Doyen of Welsh historians, the late Glanmor Williams, published his *Wales and the Reformation* in 1997. After something of a lull during the 1990s, Lloyd George studies have conspicuously revived and led to the appearance of several seminal volumes in the new millennium, including key works by John Campbell, Richard Toye, Ffion Hague, Lord (Roy) Hattersley and Travis Crosby. The *Welsh Academy Dictionary*, the result of the herculean labours of Bruce Griffiths and Dafydd Glyn Jones, published back in 1995, has been buttressed by the appearance in 2002 of the last volume of *Geiriadur Prifysgol Cymru*, the culmination of eight long decades of dedicated scholarship. The dictionary staff then turned to the revision of the early instalments of this mammoth work. And, in 2007, there appeared the majestic twin volumes *Gwyddoniadur Cymru* and *The Encyclopaedia of Wales*, meticulously edited by Menna Baines, Nigel Jenkins, John Davies and Peredur I. Lynch, a veritable treasure trove of facts and figures relating to contemporary Wales and its past.

Publishing continues to flourish throughout Wales, with Gwasg Gomer (Llandysul), Y Lolfa (Talybont) and Gwasg Carreg Gwalch (Llanrwst), which have all invested heavily in the latest technological advances in their printing presses, at the forefront of publishing in the two languages of Wales. Each of these publishing houses produces a formidable torrent of works, and is aided by the ready practical support and wise counsel of the flourishing Welsh Books Council. Welsh publications such as the weekly *Y Cymro* and *Golwg* and the bi-monthly *Barn* continue to prosper, all widely read in different parts of Wales, while several Anglo-Welsh publications like *Planet* and the *New Welsh Review* remain respected and influential. A remarkable array of Welsh academic journals, including the transactions of the resilient county and local history societies in Wales, continue to flourish mightily in our little land. The enterprising innovation of the Learned Society of Wales was founded in May 2010, and soon attracted the support of a distinguished array of fellows and supporters from all parts of Wales.

# Important Dates

| | |
|---|---|
| **43** | **Roman Conquest of Britain began** |
| 47 | Roman attack on 'Wales' |
| *c.* 400 | Cunedda moves from Scotland to Wales |
| 547 | Death of Maelgwn Gwynedd |
| *c.* 768 | Welsh Church conforms to Roman usages |
| *c.* 784 | Offa of Mercia constructs Offa's Dyke |
| **802–39** | **Egbert, King of Wessex, overlord of England** |
| 844–78 | Rhodri Mawr, King of Wales |
| 871–99 | Alfred, King of Wessex |
| *c.* 900–50 | Hywel Dda, King of Wales |
| 1039–63 | Gruffydd ap Llywelyn unites Wales |
| **1066** | **Battle of Hastings: William of Normandy becomes King of England (1066–87)** |
| 1075–96 | Rhys ap Tewdwr rules south Wales |
| 1090 | Normans begin to conquer south Wales |
| 1137–70 | Owain Gwynedd rules |
| 1143 | Cistercians found Whitland Abbey |
| 1170–97 | The Lord Rhys rules south Wales |
| 1196–1240 | Reign of Llywelyn ab Iorwerth (Llywelyn 'the Great') |
| **1215** | **Magna Carta signed by King John of England** |
| 1246–82 | Reign of Llywelyn ap Gruffydd, 'The Last Prince' |
| 1267 | Treaty of Montgomery: Llywelyn recognized as Prince of Wales |
| **1272–1307** | **Edward I** |
| 1276–7 | First 'War of Welsh Independence' |
| 1277 | Treaty of Aberconwy: Llywelyn humiliated |
| 1282–3 | Second 'War of Welsh Independence' |

| | |
|---|---|
| 1282 | Death of Llywelyn at Cilmeri |
| 1283 | Death of his brother Prince Dafydd; Edward I's castle-building programme in Wales begins |
| 1284 | Statute of Wales by Edward I |
| 1294 | Revolt of Madog ap Llywelyn |
| 1316 | Rebellion of Llywelyn Bren |
| 1400–15 | Revolt of Owain Glyndŵr |
| **1455** | **Wars of the Roses begin in England** |
| 1471 | Edward IV's Council of Welsh Marches at Ludlow |
| 1485 | Henry Tudor lands in Pembroke and marches to Bosworth |
| **1492** | **Columbus sails to America** |
| **1536–8** | **Dissolution of monasteries** |
| 1536–43 | Union legislation |
| 1546 | First printed book in Welsh: *Yn y Lhyvyr Hwnn* |
| 1567 | Translation of Prayer Book and New Testament into Welsh |
| 1582 | Iron smelting near Neath |
| **1588** | **Defeat of Spanish Armada** |
| 1588 | Complete Welsh Bible translated by Bishop William Morgan |
| 1591 | Martyrdom of Puritan John Penry |
| 1639 | First Puritan congregation in Wales convened at Llanfaches in Gwent |
| **1642** | **Civil War begins in England** |
| 1644 | Battle of Montgomery: first battle of the Civil War in Wales |
| 1647 | Fall of Harlech Castle, last Royalist fortress |
| 1648 | Second Civil War; Cromwell in Wales |
| **1649** | **Charles I executed** |
| 1650–3 | Act for Propagation of Gospel in Wales |
| **1660** | **Charles II restored to throne** |
| 1660 | Restoration of the Council of Wales |
| 1674 | Schools of the Welsh Trust |
| 1689 | Abolition of the Council of Wales |
| 1699 | Society for the Promotion of Christian Knowledge |

| | |
|---|---|
| 1707 | Edward Lhuyd's *Archaeologia Britannica*: foundation of Celtic studies |
| 1718 | First printing press on Welsh soil, at Trefhedyn, Cardiganshire |
| 1735 | Conversion of Howel Harris |
| *c.* 1737–61 | Circulating schools of Griffith Jones |
| 1743 | Methodist Association in Wales |
| 1751 | Cymmrodorion Society formed in London |
| 1755 | Brecknockshire Agricultural Society founded |
| 1757 | Isaac Wilkinson starts industry at Hirwaun |
| 1759 | Guest begins to develop Merthyr Tydfil industry |
| 1762 | Second Methodist revival |
| **1776** | **American Declaration of Independence** |
| 1777 | Bacon develops industry in Merthyr |
| 1782 | Pennant inherits Penrhyn estate; Caernarfonshire slate industry launched |
| 1785 | Thomas Charles of Bala's circulating schools begun |
| **1789** | **French Revolution begins** |
| 1793–4 | Cardiff to Merthyr canal constructed |
| 1794 | Richard Crawshay buys Cyfarthfa iron works Morgan John Rhys emigrates to the USA |
| 1797 | French revolutionary fleet lands at Fishguard |
| 1801 | First census: Welsh population is 587,000 |
| 1811 | Separation of Welsh Methodists from Church of England |
| **1815** | **Battle of Waterloo** |
| 1830 | Abolition of the Courts of Great Sessions |
| 1831 | Merthyr Riots |
| **1832** | **Great Reform Act at Westminster** |
| **1837** | **Accession of Queen Victoria** |
| 1839 | Chartist attack on Newport |
| 1839–44 | Rebecca Riots |
| 1847 | Publication of the 'Blue Books' report on Wales |
| **1854** | **Outbreak of Crimean War** |
| 1859 | Liberal victories at elections; evictions of tenants Welsh religious revival |

| | |
|---|---|
| **1861–5** | **American Civil War** |
| 1865 | Welsh colony in Patagonia founded |
| 1868 | Liberal victories in Welsh seats in election |
| 1872 | Opening of the University College of Wales, Aberystwyth |
| 1881 | Passage of Welsh Sunday Closing Act |
| 1883 | Opening of University College, Cardiff |
| 1884 | Opening of the University College of North Wales, Bangor |
| 1885 | Welsh Language Society founded by Dan Isaac Davies |
| 1886 | *Cymru Fydd* movement formed |
| | Tithe War in north and west Wales |
| 1889 | Welsh Intermediate Education Act |
| 1890 | Election of Lloyd George as MP for Caernarfon Boroughs |
| 1893–6 | Royal Commission on Land in Wales |
| 1893 | Charter to federal University of Wales |
| 1896 | Central Welsh Board set up |
| 1898 | Foundation of South Wales Miners' Federation |
| 1900 | Election of Keir Hardie as Labour MP for Merthyr Tydfil |
| 1904 | Religious revival led by Evan Roberts |
| 1907 | Foundation of National Library, National Museum and Welsh Board of Education |
| 1910 | Tonypandy Riots |
| 1914 | Act to Disestablish the Church in Wales |
| **1914–18** | **First World War** |
| 1916 | Lloyd George becomes Prime Minister |
| 1920 | Church Disestablishment |
| | Opening of University College, Swansea |
| 1922 | *Urdd Gobaith Cymru* (Welsh League of Youth) formed |
| 1925 | *Plaid Genedlaethol Cymru* (Welsh Nationalist Party) founded |
| 1926 | Miners' strike; General Strike |
| 1936 | Burning of bombing school in Llŷn |
| **1939–45** | **Second World War** |

| | |
|---|---|
| 1946 | St Fagan's Castle to be Welsh Folk Museum |
| 1951 | Minister for Welsh Affairs appointed |
| 1955 | Cardiff declared official capital of Wales |
| 1962 | *Cymdeithas yr Iaith Gymraeg* (Welsh Language Society) formed |
| | Welsh Books Council set up |
| 1964 | James Griffiths appointed first Secretary of State for Wales |
| 1966 | Election of Gwynfor Evans as Plaid Cymru MP for Carmarthen |
| | Aberfan disaster |
| 1967 | Welsh Language Act passed |
| 1973 | Kilbrandon Commission report recommends assembly for Wales |
| 1974 | Local government reorganization |
| 1979 | Referendum on Welsh assembly |
| 1982 | Welsh-language television channel (S4C) set up |
| **1984–5** | **Miners' strike** |
| 1988 | Welsh Language Board set up as a consultative body |
| 1991 | Census reveals an increase in the population of Wales to 2,890,000 and an increase in the proportion of schoolchildren able to speak the Welsh language |
| 1992 | Unemployment reaches 10 per cent in Wales |
| | Neil Kinnock resigns as the leader of the Labour Party following his party's defeat in the general election |
| 1993 | Welsh Language Act passed; Welsh Language Board re-established as a statutory body with Lord Elis-Thomas as chairman |
| 1996 | Local government reorganization: 22 unified authorities succeed the 8 county councils and all district councils |
| 1997 | General Election: Labour wins 34 of the 40 redistributed Welsh constituencies; Conservatives lose all Welsh seats; Ron Davies becomes the new Secretary of State for Wales |
| | September referendum leads to a tiny majority in |

favour of a Welsh national assembly to be established in 1999

**1999**    **First elections to the National Assembly for Wales held on 6 May**

Objective One funding secured for deprived areas in Wales

Opening of the Millennium Stadium in Cardiff

2000    Rhodri Morgan becomes the First Minister of Wales

2001    Census figures reveal small increase in the proportion of Welsh speakers

2002    Completion of *Geiriadur Prifysgol Cymru* (the University of Wales Dictionary)

2004    Richard Commission report published in March

Millennium Centre opened in Cardiff Bay in November

Katherine Jenkins records her first CD

2006    New Senedd building opened by Queen Elizabeth II on St David's Day; Government of Wales Act awards increased powers to the National Assembly

2007    Simultaneous publication of *Gwyddoniadur Cymru* and *The Encyclopaedia of Wales*

2008    Closure of the Tower colliery, Hirwaun, in March, the last deep coal mine in Wales

2009    St David's Centre in Cardiff re-opened in November

2010    Unemployment in Wales runs at 9.2 per cent

2011    Referendum on law-making powers for the National Assembly has a positive outcome on 3 March; census returns reveal population of Wales is now 3.1 million people

# Further Reading

A major renaissance in Welsh historical studies has taken place ever since the 1960s. The fruits of this are perhaps best reflected in the splendid volumes of the Oxford History of Wales, published jointly by the Clarendon Press, Oxford, and the University of Wales Press. Five volumes have appeared to date:

Thomas Charles Edwards, *Wales and the Britons, 350–1064* (2012).
R.R. Davies, *Conquest, Coexistence and Change: Wales 1063–1415* (1986).
Glanmor Williams, *Recovery, Reorientation and Reformation: Wales c.1415–1642* (1987).
Geraint H. Jenkins, *The Foundations of Modern Wales: Wales 1642–1780* (1987).
Kenneth O. Morgan, *Rebirth of a Nation: Wales 1880–1980* (1981).

Other general works of great merit are:
Glanmor Williams, *The Welsh Church from Conquest to Reformation* (2nd edn, 1976).
David Williams, *A History of Modern Wales* (2nd edn, 1977).
Kenneth O. Morgan, *Wales in British Politics, 1868–1922* (3rd edn, 1980).
A.J. Roderick (ed.), *Wales through the Ages* (2 vols, 1959 and 1960).
Hugh Thomas. *A History of Wales, 1485–1660* (1972).
E.D. Evans, *A History of Wales, 1660–1815* (1976).
Wendy Davies, *Wales in the Early Middle Ages* (1982).

Prys Morgan and David Thomas, *Wales: the Shaping of a Nation* (1984).

Dai Smith, *Wales! Wales!* (1984).

Gwyn A. Williams, *When was Wales? A History of the Welsh* (1985).

D. Gareth Evans, *A History of Wales, 1815–1906* (1989).

John Davies, *Hanes Cymru* (1990).

David Walker, *Medieval Wales* (1990)

John Davies, *A History of Wales* (1993)

R. R. Davies, *The Revolt of Owain Glyn Dŵr* (1997)

Glanmor Williams, *Wales and the Reformation* (1997)

D. Gareth Evans, *A History of Wales, 1906–2000* (2000).

Geraint H. Jenkins, *A Concise History of Wales* (2006).

Gerald Morgan, *A Brief History of Wales* (2008).

John Gower, *The Story of Wales* (2012).

Among the numerous guides to archaeological sites and ancient monuments are:

W.T. Barber, *The Visitors' Guide to Historic Places of Wales* (1984).

*An Illustrated Guide to the Ancient Monuments of Wales* (1973).

Two extraordinarily useful works of reference are:

*The Dictionary of Welsh Biography down to 1940* (1959).

Meic Stephens (ed.), *The Oxford Companion to the Literature of Wales* (1986, revised and published as *The New Companion to the Literature of Wales* by the University of Wales Press 1998).

The seven volumes in the Welsh History and its Sources Series, edited by Trevor Herbert and Gareth Elwyn Jones, each provide an admirable introduction to the periods covered:

*Edward I and Wales* (1988).

*Tudor Wales* (1988).

*The Remaking of Wales in the Eighteenth Century* (1988).

*People and Protest: Wales, 1815–1880* (1988).

*Wales 1880–1914* (1988).

*Wales between the Wars* (1988).

*Post-War Wales* (1995)

These volumes comprise a useful selection of source materials vividly illustrating many of the themes discussed in this book.

The monumental publication of *The Encyclopaedia of Wales* in English and *Gwyddoniadur Cymru* in Welsh, edited by Menna Baines, Nigel Jenkins, John Davies and Peredur I. Lynch, took place in 2008.

*Welsh Biography Online* continues today as the successor to the *Dictionary of Welsh Biography*, hosted at the National Library of Wales.

The Pevsner Architectural Guides series to the Buildings of Wales was completed in 2009, comprising the volumes that now cover the whole of Wales:
*Powys: Montgomeryshire, Radnorshire and Breconshire* (1979; 2013)
*Clwyd (Denbighshire and Flintshire)* (1986)
*Glamorgan* (1995)
*Gwent/Monmouthshire* (2000)
*Pembrokeshire* (2004)
*Carmarthenshire and Ceredigion* (2006)
*Gwynedd* (2009)

# Glossary of Terms

*Aberfan disaster* On 21 October 1966 part of a coal-tip slid into the Aberfan valley near Merthyr Tydfil, crushing houses and burying the Pant-glas Junior School; 116 children and 28 adults lost their lives.

*Aberffraw* A village in the south-west of Anglesey and the chief court of the Princes of Gwynedd. From 1230 Llywelyn ab Iorwerth used the title 'Prince of Aberffraw and Lord of Snowdon'.

*Arian* A believer in the doctrine of Arius of Alexandria who denied the full divinity of Christ.

*Arminian* A holder of the doctrine of Arminius, a Dutch Protestant theologian who opposed the views of Calvin, especially on predestination. Arminians emphasized the doctrine and worship of the early Church and were suspected of trying to reintroduce Roman Catholicism.

*Bondsman* The unfree peasant of the Middle Ages, personally bound to his lord and providing services and dues in return for his holding, an arrangement ordered by Welsh customary law. They lived either in a *maerdref* (demesne vill) or a *tir-cyfrif* (manorial vill), and provided labour for the prince or lord of the commote.

*Cantref* An administrative, judicial and territorial unit of medieval Wales, consisting in theory of a hundred townships. From the eleventh century they were divided into commotes.

*Commote* or *Cwmwd* A sub-division of the cantref. Each had its court of justice, its machinery and officials for the supervision of the bond villages and the collection of tribal dues.

*Cymanfa ganu* A singing festival, a prominent feature of

215

Nonconformist worship in Wales. They were held from about 1830 and became more popular from the 1860s, often developing on denominational lines.

*Cymru Fydd* The Young Wales movement, founded by Welshmen in London in 1886 on the model of Young Ireland. Its many branches were to be found in most parts of Wales. Home Rule was central to its programme. It collapsed after 1896.

*Deist* A believer in the existence of a god without accepting revelation.

*Demesne* Land kept in the hands of the lord, often worked by bondsmen to supply the lord's arable requirements.

*Denizen* A foreigner admitted to residence and granted certain rights and privileges.

*Eisteddfod* A festival of cultural activities, usually organized on competitive lines. The tradition dates from at least the fifteenth century, perhaps from 1176. It was revived as a national event during the nineteenth century.

*Feudal system* A medieval European form of government based on the relation of vassal and superior arising from the holding of lands in feud or fief.

*Fief* The sphere of operation or control of a lord.

*Gorsedd Beirdd Ynys Prydain* A society of poets, musicians and other representatives of Welsh culture, founded by Iolo Morganwg in 1792. Its activities are usually confined to the ceremonies of the National Eisteddfod.

*Gwely* Clan land, held by both bond and free communities, generally subject to partible succession at the death of a clansman.

*Homage and fealty* The personal submission of a tenant to his lord, whereby the tenant was bound to serve his lord and the lord to warrant his tenant.

*Maenor* Manor; a social and tenurial organization comprising a lord, free and unfree tenants. *Maenorau* varied infinitely in their size and organization.

*McKinley tariff* A duty imposed by the United States government in 1891 in an attempt to foster a tinplate industry at home. Its imposition soon led to a crisis in the Welsh industry and mass unemployment.

*Oath-helpers* Those who supported by oath the oath of the defendant denying the accusation. They originally came from the kinsfolk of the accused, but it was later laid down that they should be men of the same rank as the accused but unrelated.

*Parliamenta* A term used from the 1240s to describe important assemblies of the king and his nobles to discuss military, financial, judicial and domestic affairs or foreign policy.

*Partible inheritance* The division of the deceased's estate amongst all his heirs – sometimes known as gavelkind.

*Patrimony* Property inherited from one's father or ancestors' heritage.

*Pluralism* The holding of more than one office, especially clergyman's benefice, at a time.

*Primogeniture* The right of succession belonging to the first-born alone, especially the passage of the patrimony of the deceased to the eldest son in feudal rule.

*Rebecca* The Rebecca rioters took their text from a verse in the Book of Genesis, Chapter 24, 60, 'And they blessed Rebekah and said unto her, Let thy seed possess the gates of those which hate thee'. Each band of rioters had its Rebecca, its leader for the occasion, a man who was often disguised as a woman, but although a number have been identified, it has proved impossible to establish a single overall leader.

*Scotch Cattle* Bands of workers who in the valleys of south-east Wales from 1820 to 1835 attacked those against whom they had grievances or amongst whom they were determined to enforce solidarity. The area of their operations was known as the Black Domain.

*Spencer Unions* Independent trade unions, initially centred on the coalfields in the English Midlands, which lay outside the control of, and were generally antagonistic to, the South Wales Miners' Federation.

*Uchelwyr* The native Welsh aristocratic class.

*Unitarian* A Christian who denies the doctrine of the Trinity and the deity of Jesus Christ. Within Wales the movement has been strongest in south Cardiganshire and north Carmarthenshire. The Unitarians were noted for their Radical tendencies in the late eighteenth and early nineteenth centuries.

# Index

The History of Wales

The History of Wales

Newport 87, 118, 120, 121, 125, 149, 175, 178, 195, 201, 207
Newtown 120, 123, 164
Nichol, William 62
Nicholas, Jemima 106–7
Normans 17–27
*North Wales Chronicle* 128
North Wales Quarrymen's Union 136
Northumberland, Earl of 49

Objective One funding 187
Observations on the Nature of Civil Liberty 104, 105
Ocean Coal Company 119–20
Offa 13
Offa's Dyke 13–14, 21
Ogam 9, 10
Owain Glyndŵr 23, 40, 45, 47–50, 52, 53, 61, 140, 203
Owain Gwynedd 21, 22, 25, 27
Owain Lawgoch 45
Owen, Albert 189
Owen, David (Brutus) 128
Owen, Gerallt Lloyd 180
Owen, Goronwy 100
Owen, Sir Hugh 137, 138, 140
Owen, Sir John, of Clenennau 80
Owen, Robert 123, 124

*Pages from Memory* 172
Paine, Tom 106
Palaeolithic period 1
*papurau bro* 183
Parliament for Wales Campaign (1950s) 170
Parry, Gwenlyn 180
Parry, R. Williams 180
Parry, Bishop Richard 75
Parry-Williams, Sir T. H. 180
Patagonia 115, 143, 144
Pengwern 10
Penmaen-mawr 4
Pennal policy 49
Pennant, Richard, Lord Penrhyn 116, 136
Penry, John 63
Pentre Ifan 2, 3
Penyberth 157
Penydarren ironworks 118
Percy, Henry 48
periodical press 128–9
Philipps, Sir John, Picton Castle 91, 92
Phillips, Morgan 156
Phillips, Sir Thomas 139
Picts 8
*Plaid Genedlaethol Cymru* (later *Plaid Cymru*) 156, 157, 161, 168, 169, 170,

172, 173, 174, 175, 176, 186, 189–92, 194
*Planet* 181, 204
Plebs League 147
Plymouth ironworks 118
*Poetry Wales* 181
Pollitt, Harry 161
Pontypridd 111, 158, 175, 183
Poor Law Amendment Act (1834) 113, 124
*Portrait of the Artist as a Young Dog* 181
pottery industry 116
Powell, Rice 80, 81
Powell, Vavasor 77–8, 81, 82, 83
Powys, mediaeval kingdom of 9–10, 12, 14–16, 19, 21, 22, 27, 30, 31, 34, 48
Poyer, John 81
Presbyterian College 138, 144
Price, Adam 189
Price, Dr Hugh 70
Price, Dr Richard 104, 105, 106
Prichard, Rees 76
Prys, Edmwnd 63, 64, 75, 76
Pryse family of Gogerddan 69, 86
Pryse, Lewis, of Gogerddan 103
Puritanism 63, 64, 77–8, 79, 81–4, 86, 99–100
purveyance 74

Quakers 84, 85, 158

Railways 109, 114, 118, 119, 120, 121, 133, 143, 147, 148, 149, 152, 155, 163, 165, 200
Ratepayers party 168
Rebecca Riots 113–14, 127
Recusants 64–5, 79
Redwood, John 175, 176
Rees, Thomas (Twm Carnabwth) 114
Rees, William (Gwilym Hiraethog) 128, 143
Referendum on Welsh devolution (1979) 173
Referendum on Welsh devolution (1997) 177, 185
Reform Act (1832) 124, 127
Reform Act (1867) 128, 131, 144
Reform Act (1884) 134, 144, 145
Reformation 59–64
Representation of the People Act (1948) 168
Rhiwlas estate 130
Rhodri Mawr 14–15
Rhondda 117, 119, 120–2, 136, 146, 147, 155, 161, 166, 170, 180, 186
Rhuddlan, Statute of (1284) 37, 55
Rhydderch ap Iestyn 16
Rhys ap Gruffudd 22